More Praise for *Better Together*

This is a must-read book for several reasons: It's the first of its kind on a new, increasing wave of church mergers built on vision rather than survival. It's based on real-life, first-hand research based on real church mergers by two of Christianity's most respected voices. It develops a common language that subsequent conversations about church mergers can build upon, and the authors walk the reader through the various steps to a successful church merger."
—Dr. Bill Easum, president, 21st Century Strategies, Inc.,
www.effectivechurch.com; coauthor, *Ten Most
Common Mistakes Made by Church Starts*

"Tomberlin and Bird have knocked the ball out of the park in this book. The research is incredible, the content is insightful and the net results are invaluable. Considering the trends, this book is a must-read for church leaders serious about making the most of what God gives them."
—Dan Reiland, executive pastor, 12Stone Church,
Lawrenceville, Georgia; author, *Amplified Leadership*

"The church merger process that has been instinctively used in the past . . . has failed. And it will continue to fail. If a merger is at all in your thinking, please read this book. There is a right way . . . and you'll find it here!"
—W. Charles Arn, president, Church Growth Inc.; Monrovia, California;
author, *Heartbeat: How to Turn Passion into Ministry*

"This book addresses the most common challenges related to church mergers. Having planted several churches as well as having experienced the complicated task of a church merger, this is a must-read. You can choose to travel this road alone, but take my advice, it's always easier, faster, and 'better together.'"
—Jaime Loya, senior pastor, Valley International
Christian Center, San Benito, Texas

"An essential resource for any mission-driven church considering a merger. Practical, field-tested strategies that will help leaders avoid common pitfalls. I highly recommend it!"
—Jonathan Schaeffer, senior pastor, Grace Church,
Middleburg Heights, Ohio

"We *need* this kind of win-win thinking in the church. I'd love it if denominational leaders were thinking this way. (I wonder if a challenge needs to go out to them explicitly!) I don't know of any resource like this in print. *Better Together* will stimulate a wave of kingdom impact that will make us all say 'Why didn't we think of this sooner?'"
—Mark Ashton, senior pastor, Christ Community
Church, Omaha, Nebraska

"Today's congregational leaders often wonder whether "going it alone" is their best option. Yet the "m-word" (merger) can elicit tremendous fear, confusion, and disappointment—both when the negotiations succeed and when they don't. This book offers clear and thoughtful guidance about the how and the why (and even the 'Why not?') of merger initiatives. Serious study of this material will move leaders miles ahead in their thinking and will greatly increase the chances that a robust and renewed ministry will result from a merger initiative."

—Alice Mann, consultant, The Alban Institute; author,
Can Our Church Live?

"Jim Tomberlin and Warren Bird have bent my mind again. Like many, I was mired in the old math of church mergers—and now I see that mergers, done well, offer a powerful way to expand God's kingdom. *Better Together* is ahead of its time. It's thorough and inspirational without being laborious. Thank you, Jim and Warren, for pushing me in this direction!"

—Dr. Tom Nebel, director of Church Planting, Converge
Worldwide, Orlando, Florida

"*Better Together* is a practical and complete guide to an emerging opportunity to reclaim and maximize kingdom resources. Don't attempt to even consider a merger without taking advantage of their research."

—Steve Stroope, lead pastor, Lake Pointe Church,
Rockwall, Texas; author, *Tribal Church* and *It Starts at Home*

"Opportunities for churches working together have never existed like they exist now, but only those who are alert and aware of these strategies will take advantage of this connection. Merging churches takes help and expertise, and this book is a powerful guide to jumpstart such an endeavor."

—Rick Bezet, lead pastor, New Life Church, Central Arkansas

"In a church I previously served, I initiated a merger. Ours was the joining church, and we became part of a stronger church in my community. We did many of the things this book recommends. It was the best thing to do for my church and for the kingdom of God. God really blessed the merger."

—Rod Layman, pastor, First Baptist Church, Mesa, Arizona

"When I began consulting twenty-four years ago church mergers were normally based on two dying churches coming together for survival. Not so any more. Tomberlin and Bird show that today's most successful mergers are mission-driven as two (or more) churches come together around a compelling vision. . . . *Better Together* will become a definitive guidebook. Out of a complex and emerging landscape, Tomberlin and Bird have distilled useful principles and provided a new vocabulary of family-related terms to use. We are speaking of our own merger as a 'marriage' because we envision 'having kids together' through new ministry sites in the future."

—Rev. Dr. Christopher M. Ritter, directing pastor,
First United Methodist Church, Geneseo, Illinois

"Tomberlin and Bird give us a great resource to help churches join together for a greater impact. Having experienced a church merger firsthand, I'm convinced it's worth the journey. Here's a guidebook to help you along the path."

—Tony Morgan, strategist, www.TonyMorganLive.com;
coauthor, *Killing Cockroaches: And Other Scattered Musings on Leadership*

"Tomberlin and Bird rightly describe a growing movement among churches learning to walk, work, and worship God together as one; churches rejecting competition for cooperation and working smart not hard. As one who has both led and benefitted from church mergers, I invite you to prayerfully consider this practical guide."

—Dr. Mark DeYmaz, pastor, Mosaic Church, Little Rock,
Arkansas; author, *Building a Healthy Multi-Ethnic Church*

International Praise for *Better Together*

"Jim Tomberlin and Warren Bird are on to something very important. As they point out, you don't have to use the word *merger*. Regardless of what you call it, the concept is similar to church planting and has tremendous potential to expand the impact of vibrant churches as well as revitalize declining churches."

—Nicky Gumbel, senior vicar, Holy Trinity Church Brompton,
London; founder, Alpha Course

"God is rewiring his church to reach a new generation. *Better Together* is an invaluable resource to any church considering a merger. It is comprehensive, well researched, practical, and insightful. We pastor at a multisite church that has successfully grown through a merger and can say, 'Tomberlin and Bird get it!' Mergers have great potential. They also come with potential pitfalls. This book will help ensure both churches involved are truly better together."

—Bruxy Cavey, teaching pastor, and Tim Day, senior pastor,
The Meeting House, Oakville, Ontario, Canada

"Jim Tomberlin and Warren Bird have provided the church with a visionary and practical book from which, if many church leaders could embrace it with real humility, the kingdom impact could be huge. Whether you lead a thriving church or are involved in one that is struggling, I commend this book to you."

—Steve Tibbert, senior pastor, King's Church, London, England; author, *Good to Grow*

"This book is a treasure trove of gems, practical tips on how to navigate the rough seas of merging a church and some small things that can have a major impact. If we had this book fifteen years ago when we had undergone such an endeavour, it would not have been so painful for a lot of people, and we would have been able to avoid many of the pitfalls we have found ourselves in. I can recommend this book to any church considering embarking on such a journey."

—Dr. Johan Geyser, cultural architect, Mosaïek Church, Johannesburg, South Africa

"Jim Tomberlin and Warren Bird have always been great at understanding what the next move is in church culture. With *Better Together—Making Church Mergers Work* they have brought the topic of mergers to a wider audience. Church mergers are not only relevant in the United States, but also in Europe with huge church-planting implications. It's a must-read book for church leaders who are strategic thinkers."

—ND Strupler, executive director, ICF Movement, Zurich, Switzerland

"The book is extremely helpful in understanding that good mergers actually increase the kingdom of God—including the total number of churches because they become vehicles of change, not preservers of the status quo. Mergers may not be what church leaders had in mind for their churches when they started them, but they may indeed be God's key to open doors to new opportunities of greater harvest. For those local churches considering a merger, *Better Together* contains lots of practical wisdom that would lead to peril if not heeded."

—Dr. Dietrich Schindler, executive director, Church Planting, Evangelical Free Church, Germany

"Much like blended families, church mergers are becoming more frequent in our generation. Thanks to *Better Together*, we now have an excellent guide to assist us in avoiding the land mines and maximizing the potential of this unfamiliar territory."

—Mark Conner, senior minister, CityLife Church, Victoria, Australia

Better Together

Making Church Mergers Work

Jim Tomberlin
and
Warren Bird

Foreword by Craig Groeschel

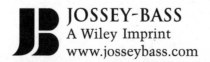

JOSSEY-BASS
A Wiley Imprint
www.josseybass.com

Published by Jossey-Bass A Wiley Imprint One Montgomery Street, Suite 1200, San Francisco, CA 94104-4594—www.josseybass.com

Jossey-Bass books and products are available through most bookstores. To contact Jossey-Bass directly call our Customer Care Department within the U.S. at 800-956-7739, outside the U.S. at 317-572-3986, or fax 317-572-4002.

Wiley publishes in a variety of print and electronic formats and by print-on-demand. Some material included with standard print versions of this book may not be included in e-books or in print-on-demand. If this book refers to media such as a CD or DVD that is not included in the version you purchased, you may download this material at http://booksupport.wiley.com. For more information about Wiley products, visit www.wiley.com.

Library of Congress Cataloging-in-Publication Data

Tomberlin, Jim, author.
    Better together : making church mergers work / Jim Tomberlin and Warren Bird ; Foreword by Craig Groeschel.—First edition.
        pages cm.—(Jossey-Bass leadership network series ; 62)
    Includes index.
    ISBN 978-1-118-13130-5 (hardback); 978-1-118-21819-8 (ebk); 978-1-118-21820-4 (ebk); 978-1-118-21821-1 (ebk)
    1. Christian union. I. Bird, Warren, author. II. Title.
BX8.3.T66 2012
262'.2—dc23

                                                                                          2011047500

Printed in the United States of America

FIRST EDITION
HB Printing   10 9 8 7 6

Leadership Network Titles

The Blogging Church: Sharing the Story of Your Church Through Blogs, Brian Bailey and Terry Storch

Church Turned Inside Out: A Guide for Designers, Refiners, and Re-Aligners, Linda Bergquist and Allan Karr

Leading from the Second Chair: Serving Your Church, Fulfilling Your Role, and Realizing Your Dreams, Mike Bonem and Roger Patterson

In Pursuit of Great AND Godly Leadership: Tapping the Wisdom of the World for the Kingdom of God, Mike Bonem

Hybrid Church: The Fusion of Intimacy and Impact, Dave Browning

The Way of Jesus: A Journey of Freedom for Pilgrims and Wanderers, Jonathan S. Campbell with Jennifer Campbell

Cracking Your Church's Culture Code: Seven Keys to Unleashing Vision and Inspiration, Samuel R. Chand

Leading the Team-Based Church: How Pastors and Church Staffs Can Grow Together into a Powerful Fellowship of Leaders, George Cladis

Organic Church: Growing Faith Where Life Happens, Neil Cole

Church 3.0: Upgrades for the Future of the Church, Neil Cole

Journeys to Significance: Charting a Leadership Course from the Life of Paul, Neil Cole

Off-Road Disciplines: Spiritual Adventures of Missional Leaders, Earl Creps

Reverse Mentoring: How Young Leaders Can Transform the Church and Why We Should Let Them, Earl Creps

Building a Healthy Multi-Ethnic Church: Mandate, Commitments, and Practices of a Diverse Congregation, Mark DeYmaz

Leading Congregational Change Workbook, James H. Furr, Mike Bonem, and Jim Herrington

The Tangible Kingdom: Creating Incarnational Community, Hugh Halter and Matt Smay

Baby Boomers and Beyond: Tapping the Ministry Talents and Passions of Adults over Fifty, Amy Hanson

Leading Congregational Change: A Practical Guide for the Transformational Journey, Jim Herrington, Mike Bonem, and James H. Furr

The Leader's Journey: Accepting the Call to Personal and Congregational Transformation, Jim Herrington, Robert Creech, and Trisha Taylor

Contents

About the Jossey-Bass Leadership Network Series

Leadership Network's mission is to accelerate the impact of OneHundredX leaders. These high-capacity leaders are like the hundredfold crop that comes from seed planted in good soil as Jesus described in Matthew 13:8.

Leadership Network . . .

- Explores the "what's next?" of what could be
- Creates "aha!" environments for collaborative discovery
- Works with exceptional "positive deviants"
- Invests in the success of others through generous relationships
- Pursues big impact through measurable kingdom results
- Strives to model Jesus through all we do

Believing that meaningful conversations and strategic connections can change the world, we seek to help leaders navigate the future by exploring new ideas and finding application for each unique context. Through collaborative meetings and processes, leaders map future possibilities and challenge one another to action that accelerates fruitfulness and effectiveness. Leadership Network shares the learnings and inspiration with others through our books, concept papers, research reports, e-newsletters, podcasts, videos, and online experiences. This in turn generates a ripple effect of new conversations and further influence.

In 1996 Leadership Network established a partnership with Jossey-Bass, a Wiley Imprint, to develop a series of creative books that provide thought leadership to innovators in church ministry. Leadership Network Publications present thoroughly researched and innovative concepts from leading thinkers, practitioners, and pioneering churches.

To learn more about Leadership Network, go to www.lead net.org.

Foreword

On Thursday, December 7, 2000, two elders from a nearby church called and asked me if I'd consider becoming their pastor. Because the church I had started, LifeChurch.tv, was thriving and just about to celebrate our fifth anniversary, I didn't even consider praying about it and politely declined. To my surprise, they didn't take "no" for an answer.

The men queried again, this time asking me if I'd at least pray about it. Trying not to sound rude, I explained that I was certain God wanted me to continue with the church we started. Sensing their deep desire to find a pastor, I offered to help them find the best person to lead their church. I was shocked when they declined my offer and asked me a third time to consider becoming the pastor of their church. "Is there anything we could do to get you to consider our church?" the men asked with genuine passion. "We really feel like God led us to you."

At this point I felt a little frustrated by their persistence and said somewhat flippantly, "Well, if you want your church to become a part of ours, I'll consider that."

I'm not sure if I expected them to laugh, scoff, or walk away. I do know that I never, ever expected them to say they were open to that idea. Exactly thirty days after that initial conversation, on January 7, 2001, 89.6 percent of their church voted to merge with our church, and we became one church in two locations.

At the time, I'd never heard of a church merger before. As the years would unfold, I discovered that many churches across the world are asking the question, "Could we do more for God's glory united with another church than we are doing alone?" Now, what was unheard of before is becoming a viable and strategic option for many congregations.

Since our first partnership with that local church, we've joined forces with four other smaller churches in four different states. Even though these have all worked out well, we've stepped away from dozens of similar merger opportunities.

Over time, we've discovered that two are often better than one—but not always. Sometimes $1 + 1 = 3$. Combining the right ministries can produce better outcomes than the individual ministries could accomplish alone. But other times, $1 + (\text{the wrong}) 1 = 0$. Although healthy mergers can create a spiritual synergy greater than you can imagine, the wrong mergers are like cancer to a human body.

I'm so thankful that someone finally wrote a book to address the hidden challenges and unexpected opportunities of uniting two ministries into one. And I'm even more thankful that it wasn't just anyone, but two of the most knowledgeable men I know on this subject. Not only do I value Jim Tomberlin and Warren Bird as friends, but I'm also deeply grateful for their hearts to serve the local church. If you are considering joining forces with another church, you've picked up the right book. Read *Better Together* carefully. Read it prayerfully. And I know God will prepare you to make the right decision.

Craig Groeschel

Preface

"I think you're dead on by suggesting that church mergers will be the next 'big thing.'"

The North Carolina pastor who said these words to us has not been part of a merger—yet. He suspects his church might be a good candidate for a merger, but he wants to know more about how exactly a merger could help his church go forward, how the merger process might unfold, where to find another church that his congregation could join with, and what pitfalls he and his congregation should avoid.

He represents a new wave of Protestant church leaders, denominational and nondenominational, who are watching the merger landscape and are curious as to whether God might be leading in that direction for their church and are therefore asking, "Should there be a merger in the future of *our* church?"

We are convinced a wave is building with a new kind of mission-driven church merger that will transform the church landscape across the world. Mergers are occurring among churches of all sizes and types, and they are happening in urban centers, suburban neighborhoods, and rural communities. Such mergers reflect a growing trend where two local churches at different life stages leverage their common DNA and complementary differences to generate greater synergy for a stronger regional impact.

These new kinds of merger are not what have been typical of the past, when two struggling churches made a last-gasp effort to survive. Church-merger conversations may begin because of

Mergers today succeed largely because of a united, compelling vision that lifts a church that's stuck or on a downward slope into a new pattern of life and growth.

financial difficulties, surface through local partnerships or denominational affiliations, or become initiated by a multisite church, but mergers today succeed largely because of a united, compelling vision that lifts a church that's stuck or on a downward slope into a new pattern of life and growth.

Roughly 80 percent of the three hundred thousand Protestant churches in the United States have plateaued or are declining, and many of them are in desperate need of a vibrant ministry. Among the 20 percent of growing congregations across the United States, many are in desperate need of space. These conditions present a potential win-win for forward-thinking church leaders who believe that "we can do better together than separate," and it is revitalizing church topography.

Why This Book?

We believe *Better Together: Making Church Mergers Work* is the first book in existence to focus on church mergers—and that it is long overdue. Excellent books exist on church turnarounds, church revitalization, and when necessary even church closings. However, scant formal attention has been paid to mergers, especially ones in which at least one of the merger partners is healthy and growing.

Better Together is also the first book to offer alternatives to the old, failure-prone approach that defined a merger as the coming together of two declining churches. It is also the first book to cite and draw insight from several research projects on church mergers, which are mentioned in the book and listed in Appendix G. Throughout the book we strive to offer specific, practical, how-to advice on best practices in the merger process.

In this book we propose a common language to talk about this growing phenomenon, we identify different merger models, and we also create distinctions between a *lead* church and a *joining* church. Although the topic of church mergers is discussed in the public media, church leaders need far more than news feeds about which churches in their area are planning to merge. For those who do merge, or even want to begin such discussions, there is a desperate need for a new language to talk about the topic because so many people find the currently used terms pejorative, too businesslike, or too confusing. As Chapter One points out, many church leaders don't even like the word *merger* but to date no winning destigmatized alternative has emerged.

Although clear terminology is important, we hope the most important contributions this book makes are the stories representing numerous denominations and church sizes, hard research studies on the topic, and frontline advice of what's working and what's not.

Why Jim and Warren?

Both of us love the local church and believe passionately that God wants to use it to fulfill Jesus's command to make disciples of Jesus Christ (see Matt. 28:19–20). We each trained for ministry—Jim at Georgia State University (BA) in Atlanta and Dallas Theological Seminary (ThM), and Warren at Wheaton College (BA) and Wheaton Grad School (MA) in Wheaton, Illinois; Alliance Theological Seminary (MDiv), Nyack, New York; and Fordham University (PhD), Bronx, New York. Then we each pastored churches as lead pastors and as assisting pastors, Warren on the East Coast and Jim in the Southwest and Midwest, as well as in Europe.

Today Jim is a full-time church consultant based in Phoenix. Nationally one in three of his clients are involved in a merger. Warren, who lives outside New York City, works full time with Leadership Network, overseeing its research division that for the last five years has included study and interviews about church mergers.

Both of us are seeing more interest in church mergers with each passing year, so much so that we're convinced a book is needed. We strongly believe there is no need for everyone to invent the wheel independently of each other.

Flow of the Book

The book shows how to think about and complete a successful merger. The first section is introductory, the second is informative (descriptive), and the third instructional (prescriptive). Appendixes at the end include a checklist of steps to take in a merger, examples of frequently asked questions (FAQs) from several actual mergers, and details on several dozen churches whose merger stories we tell in the body of the book.

To help with the conversation, we propose the terms *lead church* and *joining church*, which we use from Chapter One onwards. Our sense is that every church merger involves a *lead* church and a *joining* church. The merging of churches is a delicate dance in which one leads and the other follows. Some are almost equal but most are vastly unequal in size and health. Regardless, one always *leads* and the other *follows*.

We also suggest a family-related set of terms: *rebirth mergers, adoption mergers, marriage mergers,* and *intensive care unit (ICU) mergers.* We explain and illustrate these models in Chapter Two.

A Merger in Your Future?

The day before we sent the final edits back to the publisher, an excited pastor told us about a merger that occurred almost a year previously. "It's been a phenomenal experience," he said, describing his largely Asian congregation that merged with a largely Caucasian congregation. "The merger opened up a larger mission field for us. We have become more effective at being able to reach people of all ethnicities." Indeed the congregation's origins are now about 40 percent Asian, 40 percent Anglo, and 20 percent African, Hispanic, or Middle Eastern. With obvious passion this pastor then described the roughly two hundred people who gather each Sunday. "Our church increasingly looks like what the kingdom of heaven will look like." Our response is that if this is but one of the fruits that mergers are producing, then the idea is certainly worth a serious and prayerful exploration.

If you're not already having conversations about mergers, there is a good likelihood that you will soon, whether you're on paid church staff, a lay leader, an active church member, a denominational leader, or a seminary student. As you do, we want you to bring far more faith and optimism to the discussion than what you find in the typically dismal newspaper headlines about two struggling churches being forced to merge as a desperate, last-gasp hope for survival.

Mission-driven church mergers have tremendous potential to exponentially expand the impact of strong, vibrant churches as well as to revitalize plateaued and declining churches.

Instead, by reading this book you'll see that mission-driven church mergers have tremendous potential to exponentially expand the impact of strong, vibrant churches as well as to revitalize plateaued and declining churches. Yet the journey is not without danger. There are numerous landmines to be avoided by any who embark on a merger expedition with another church. We want to help strong and struggling churches alike to know that merging is a viable option for impact and revitalization. We want to show how it can be adapted to assist vibrant churches in reaching more people. We want to give hope to leaders of stuck or struggling congregations that their church might find a second life through a successful church merger. We want your church to consider how it might do ministry *better together*.

Part One

THE NEW MERGER LANDSCAPE

1

GOD IS DOING SOMETHING NEW

Biblical Basis for Mergers

It's definitely a new day for church mergers. According to Leadership Network research, 2 percent of US Protestant churches merge annually[1]—that's six thousand congregations. More significantly, another 5 percent of churches say they have already talked about merging in the future[2]—that's fifteen thousand more. These churches—plus tens of thousands of others elsewhere around the globe—are sensing that they could fulfill their God-given mission better together than separately, and they're exploring new ways to join forces for the advancement of God's kingdom.

You may not use the word *merger*. You may call the idea a *restart, replant, partnership, adoption, collaboration, consolidation, satellite, unification, reunification,* or even something more indirect like *joining forces, repotting,*[3] or *building a legacy.*[4] Whatever label you use, the core idea is two or more churches becoming one—the combining, integrating, and unifying of people, structures, systems, and resources to achieve a common purpose: doing life and ministry together as a vibrant, healthy expression of Christ's body, the church.

However you describe them, mergers are happening with an increasing frequency. And unlike the results in previous generations, many church mergers today are producing positive growth and admirable fruit. Increasingly, they are becoming a vehicle for unifying local congregations around a shared mission that is producing more effective spiritual and social impact.

Eleven Merger Contexts

In addition, mergers are showing up in a wide variety of contexts, each situation offering a slightly different benefit. Here's our sense of the top contenders:

- As *long-established churches* merge, many enter a growth cycle marked by fresh vitality, new spiritual energy, intensified community engagement, and joyful momentum—and most important, an increase in newcomers, in decisions to follow Christ, and in baptisms.

- Other *long-established churches*, facing dim prospects about their future, are delighted to discover that a merger can translate their considerable heritage into a terrific foundation for a new or next generation.

- *New churches* that are growing and are in need of facilities are finding them through a merger with a congregation that has facilities with perhaps room to spare.

- Other *new churches* that are struggling can be merged into another church, or if there is a nearby parent church, merged back into the parent church, whether into its original campus or as a new multisite campus.

- *Churches that had formerly separated* are being reunified through mergers, having decided they can do more together than apart.

- There is a growing desire among church leaders to become more *racially and ethnically diverse*. Some are seeing mergers as a way of diversifying their church and becoming more *multiethnic*.

- *Multisite churches* report that they get one out of three of their campuses as another church merges with them and becomes one of its campuses.[5]

- *Mainline and denominational churches* are using a merger approach to assist nearby struggling congregations in their faith family, nurturing them back to health and vitality, some as long-term relationships and some as only temporary adoptions.

- Among *megachurches* almost one out of five have experienced a merger, most through a smaller church joining a larger church, but sometimes even two large churches joining.[6]

- Some *megachurches* are developing national networks mostly composed of church mergers. These megachurches have an intentional strategy that encourages and facilitates church mergers.

- An increasing number of *churches of all sizes* are seeing mergers as a way of ensuring a smooth succession transition as their pastor retires.

Future chapters will provide examples from each of these contexts. Taken together, however, mergers encompass a wide spectrum of types of churches. The range of mergers includes strong, stable, stuck, and struggling churches. Many are motivated by survival, but an increasing number identify "mission" as their primary impetus.

The range of mergers includes strong, stable, stuck, and struggling churches.

All mergers involve one church that we call the *lead church*—the church representing the dominant or primary culture that will continue through the merger—and one or more *joining churches*—whose congregations will be lifted or otherwise shaped to become more like the lead church. Sometimes the lead and joining churches are very similar in their look, feel, health, and approach to ministry, but more often there is some level of distance between them. Part of the merger process involves major transformation, sometimes on the level of a death, burial, and resurrection, for the joining church to grow into the identity of the lead church.

Is This God at Work?

In the pages ahead, we identify many logical reasons why church mergers make sense, why they are increasing, and why the results are increasingly positive. But those explanations are all secondary to our sense that God is clearly behind the momentum, especially in nations where Christianity has a long history and thus a need for revitalization of long-established churches whose life cycle is ebbing. In biblical terms, we believe mergers are another example of God doing a "new thing" (Isa. 43:19), helping existing congregations to reach new levels of unity, maturity, and the fullness of Christ (Eph. 4:13).

We believe this is congruent with God's desire for "divine makeovers" as expressed through the prophet Isaiah, "Your people will rebuild the ancient ruins and will raise up the age-old foundations; you will be called Repairer of Broken Walls, Restorer of Streets with Dwellings" (Isa. 58:12).

We affirm the idea of surfing spiritual waves that Rick Warren describes in *The Purpose Driven Church*. He points out that near the church he pastors in Southern California, people can learn a lot about surfing: how to choose the right equipment, how to use it properly, how to recognize a "surfable" wave, and how to catch a wave and ride it as long as possible. But they can't learn how to build a wave. Just like surfing is the art of riding waves that God builds, "our job as church leaders . . . is to recognize a wave of God's spirit and ride it. It is not our responsibility to *make* waves but to recognize how God is working in the world and join him in the endeavor,"[7] Warren says.

We see the incoming waves of church mergers as offering a five-way win:

- *Struggling churches now win.* Stuck and struggling churches get a fresh start in living out God's purpose for their church. As one of the participants in the Leadership Network 2011 survey of church mergers said, "Today, three years after our merger, most of us have to stop and think which church someone was a former member of."

- *Strong churches win.* Strong and stable churches gain momentum as stuck or struggling churches join them in a new chapter of life. A staff member from a church of two hundred that had a church of fifty merge with it said, "The number one reason we decided to join together was to reach our community faster and more effectively. In our opening month together we had twice as many first-time guests than the two churches had separately before the merger. Within the first two months, twelve people had made decisions for Christ. We are on the road to reaching our next two hundred. I am sure we have made mistakes, but God is at work, and that's a huge win!"

- *The body of Christ wins.* The corporate witness of the local church is stronger and better able to make disciples of Jesus Christ. As one of the churches in the same Leadership Network survey said, "We are reaching more people who are farther from God than either church was doing before the merger."

- *Local communities win.* Local communities are served better by strong vibrant congregations. Leaders of a church in the same Leadership Network survey that had experienced several mergers, all with positive outcomes to date, said, "If it is God's plan, you can do no better. All leaders from the joining churches would agree that the mergers were the best thing that could have happened to our communities."

- *The kingdom of God wins.* The kingdom of God advances and grows through vital, life-giving congregations. In one church during the first weeks after its merger, nine people were baptized. "That's more than our church baptized in the last ten years," the pastor told us. The new church also saw ten other members join in those same weeks.

Everybody wins in successful mergers. With testimonies like these (and we could cite many more), isn't the idea of mergers—by whatever term you use—something worth prayerfully and seriously exploring?

Biblical Basis for Mergers

Where do we find mergers in the Bible? The word isn't there but the concept is supported throughout Scripture. The Apostle Paul taught there is "one body, one Spirit, one hope, one Lord, one faith, one baptism, one God and Father of all" (Eph. 4:4–5). The Psalmist declared "how good and pleasant it is when God's people dwell together in unity!" (Ps. 133:1). The entire drama of the New Testament is the story of God bringing diverse groups together toward that divine reality.

Jesus talks of having "other sheep" (Gentiles) that need to be brought into the flock (John 10:16). He said that the temple should be a house of prayer for *all* nations, not just his own ethnic group (Mark 11:17). The Book of Acts demonstrates a wide variety of people groups that are all brought into one church to the point, as Paul explains later, that in Christ "there is no longer any distinction between Gentiles and Jews, circumcised and uncircumcised, barbarians, savages, slaves, and free, but Christ is all, Christ is in all" (Col. 3:11, *Good News Translation*). Paul explains how Gentiles have been "grafted" into the same vine as the Jews (Rom. 11:17), and how God "brought Jews and Gentiles together as though we were only one person . . . when he united us in peace . . . by uniting Jews and Gentiles in one body" (Eph. 2:15–16). The Church is even likened to the union of male and female when forming a marriage (Eph. 5:22–32).

God is a champion for merging—bringing diverse people together into a beautiful mosaic that reflects what heaven will look like on earth. Don't verbs like *grafting, reconciling, uniting,* and *marry* all convey the idea of merging? Jews and Gentiles, men and women, rich and poor, slave or free, traditional and contemporary, old and young, denominational and nondenominational—all are invited to join, *to merge* with his family on earth and demonstrate the power of the gospel to transform lives and to break down the walls that divide us.

We affirm that healthy churches reproduce and multiply. That's why we consult and write books on church planting and multisite ministry. We need more life-giving churches, not fewer.

We are not saying that every church should merge with another church but we are advocating that every church ought to consider merging if it would better fulfill the biblically driven mission of your church and better extend God's kingdom in your community. Merging is congruent with the heart of God, the principles of Scripture, and the ideal of more effectively using the resources God has provided.

As one pastor in Atlanta told us, "The word *partnership* has changed the life of our church. The Bible tells how Peter caught so many fish that his boat was about to sink. He called over another boat and they partnered together to capture all the blessing God was giving them. That's what happened as we came together to make a difference in this community." In his case, it was a cross-cultural partnership as his growing, predominantly African American congregation joined forces with a declining predominantly white congregation. The importance of bringing another boat alongside finds expression through many different values across Scripture, as summarized in Table 1.1.

Mergers as a Strategy for Change

Wherever churches have existed for more than a few decades, there is a potential for healthy and fruitful church mergers. Jesus said, "I will build my church and the gates of hell will not prevail against it" (Matt. 16:18). Jesus is building his church, a *prevailing* church at that. His desire for his bride is that she be healthy, unified, collaborative, and effective. All local churches—the strong, the stable, the stuck, and the struggling ones—are churches that Jesus loves.

Table 1.1   Biblical Value of Churches Being "Better Together" Through a Merger

Churches merge so that they can be more . . .

Unified	"May they be brought to complete *unity* to let the world know that you sent me and have loved them . . ." (John 17:23, emphasis added).
	"There is *one body* and one Spirit—just as you were called to one hope . . ." (Eph. 4:4, emphasis added).
Purposeful	"Being like-minded . . . *being one in spirit and purpose*" (Phil. 2:2, emphasis added).
Collaborative	Paul views each city's church as one body, such as "Paul . . . to the church of God in Corinth" (I Cor. 1:2) and "To the church of the Thessalonians in God the Father and the Lord Jesus Christ" (1 Thes. 1:1).
Harmonious	"How good and pleasant it is when brothers *live together in unity*" (Ps. 133:1, emphasis added).
	"If it is possible, as far as it depends on you, *live at peace* with everyone" (Rom. 12:18, emphasis added).
Stronger	"Two are better than one, because they have a *good return* for their work" (Eccles. 4:9, emphasis added).
Effective	"Now to each one the manifestation of the Spirit is given for the *common good*" (1 Cor 12:7, emphasis added).
Fruitful	"This is to my Father's glory, that you bear much fruit, showing yourselves to be my disciples" (John 15:8).
Externally focused	"Seek the peace and prosperity of the city to which I have carried you" (Jer. 29:7).
Healthy	"But to each one of us grace has been given as Christ apportioned it . . . to prepare God's people for works of service, to that the body of Christ may be built up until we all reach unity in the faith and knowledge of the Son of God and become mature . . ." (Eph. 4:7–13).
Reconciled	"Make every effort to keep the unity of the Spirit through the bond of peace" (Eph. 4:3).
	"Finally, brothers and sisters, rejoice! *Strive for full restoration*, encourage one another, be of one mind, live in peace. And the God of love and peace will be with you" (I Cor. 13:11, emphasis added).

	"If you are offering your gift at the altar and there remember that your brother has something against you, leave your gift there in front of the altar. *First go and be reconciled* to your brother; then come and offer your gift" (Mt. 5:23–24, emphasis added).
Humble	"Do nothing out of selfish ambition or vain conceit, but in *humility* consider each other better than yourselves" (Phil. 2:3, emphasis added).
	"Therefore, as God's chosen people, holy and dearly loved, clothe yourselves with compassion, kindness, *humility*, gentleness and patience" (Col. 3:12, emphasis added).
Redemptive	"Your people will rebuild the ancient ruins and will raise up the age old foundations; you will be called Repairer of Broken Walls, Restorer of Streets with Dwellings" (Isa. 58:12).
Like heaven	"After this I looked, and there before me was a great multitude that no one could count, from *every nation, tribe, people and language*, standing before the throne and before the Lamb" (Rev. 7:9, emphasis added).

Wherever your own church falls on that spectrum, we believe it's worth prayerfully exploring whether your church may be a potential candidate for a church merger as a means of building his church overall and extending his kingdom in new ways in this generation.

Why merge?

- To be better together than each church is individually
- To begin a new church life cycle
- To reach more people for Christ
- To make a greater difference for Christ
- To multiply your church's impact
- To better serve your local community
- To leverage the legacy and good reputation of the past
- To maximize church facilities
- To be a stronger local church
- To further extend God's kingdom

For those good things to happen, all parties in the merger have to take a risk—a step of faith with no guarantee of success. The statistics on church mergers are sobering. Mergers can be hard. Many fail. This book does not announce that all mergers now work; rather, it affirms that an increasing number of churches have found a way to make mergers work and with many experiencing amazingly good results.

Are you up to exercising faith? We Americans like contests and shows like *The Biggest Loser* because we like to root against the odds. We love it when the underdog makes it. We're drawn to success stories of people going against the odds and winning.

Many of us likewise believe that we can be the exception, entering marriage with every good hope of a meaningful, life-long relationship, even though we know the reality is that too many marriages don't make it. We take long shots on other dreams—maybe of owning our own business or rising to the top of our field, even though we know that in the final outcome only a few will actually make it.

Challenges are still present for today's mergers, but as Jesus told us, with God all things are possible (see Matt. 19:26). We believe some churches are using mergers to fulfill Christ's great commission (see Matt. 18:19–20) in ways that God is eager to bless. Is that something for you to explore? Is it the "new thing" (Isa. 43:19) that God might want to do for you?

Mergers are not a strategy for maintaining the status quo. They are a strategy for dramatic change. Is a merger possibly in *your* church's future?

> *Mergers are not a strategy for maintaining the status quo.*

The New Math of Mergers

Arizona pastor Justin Anderson experienced a three-church merger in late 2010 and early 2011. The merger tripled the size of his church and left them all with a new structure, new leadership, and new name—Redemption Church (www.redemptionaz.com). Though painful at times, Justin insists it was the right pathway to pursue. "We are better together than we were apart," Justin says. "When it comes to vision, ideas, leadership, resources, and prayer, 1 + 1 + 1 = 10."

That's the new math of mergers. And it had such a positive outcome that a year later, Redemption Church did a fourth merger. And they plan for more in the coming years.

Justin Anderson's experience with church mergers is only one of many people who report it as a big win. In a Leadership Network survey, one Ohio pastor said, "The question the merger hinged upon for us was this: 'Could we reach the next two hundred people in our community faster together or separate?' When both pastors answered 'together,' it seemed unfaithful to do anything but merge." After praying, fasting, discussing with a pastoral coach, and then obtaining highly supportive votes by both congregations and their boards, these two churches from the same denomination merged—one with an attendance of 150 and the other 55.

The survey also asked how the merger went for that church. The pastor of the joining church, who filled out the survey, ranked the experience an 8 out of a possible high of 10, stating, "Our focus was on a greater impact on our community, and we achieved that. Both churches were stronger after the merge than before." For this merged church, 1 + 1 = far more than 2.

As these two churches illustrate, new-math mergers are working across many different church sizes. Premerger attendance at the first Arizona example was two thousand. Premerger attendance at the Ohio merger was 205. But church growth, though an important barometer, is not the primary measure

Church growth, though an important barometer, is not the primary measure of a merger's success. . . . The more important measures are changed lives.

of a merger's success. Instead it's whether the merger can better achieve God's call of making disciples of Jesus Christ. In that way the more important measures are changed lives.

Serial Mergers and Merger Churches Networks

National surveys affirm that there is a definite trend since the 1990s toward a greater number of mergers. This is happening among churches of all sizes, with the typical example being in the attendance range of one hundred to two hundred after the merger.[8]

However, large churches are rapidly becoming new players in mergers, especially in multiple mergers. Some are even pursuing a pathway of intentionally adding merger after merger as a way of reaching more people and extending their impact. Most, though, are like Seattle-based Mars Hill Church, where Mark Driscoll is teaching pastor, which opened ten different new campuses between 2001 and 2011 (they refer to each campus as a *church*). Four of those churches were mergers. Mars Hill has a vision of fifty such multisite churches by 2020, a portion of which will come through mergers.

Other very large churches have created large networks of merger churches. Oklahoma-based LifeChurch.tv, where Craig Groeschel is lead pastor (who also wrote the Foreword to this book), offers three levels of how it welcomes other churches to partner with it. The broadest level is called Open, and it makes a wide range of the church's resources available at no cost to anyone who will use it in a noncommercial application to lead people to Christ. The next level is called Network, in which churches connect with LifeChurch.tv through a recurring weekend experience that features free video teaching messages. The most closely aligned level with LifeChurch.tv is called United.[9] Churches that practice this level of partnership join with LifeChurch.tv in reaching people around the globe. They become a LifeChurch.tv campus. Their pastor becomes a campus pastor of LifeChurch.tv. By late 2011 the church had fifteen different campuses, five of which came as mergers.

North Point Community Church, a church based in greater Atlanta, where Andy Stanley is senior pastor, does not use the word *merger*. Leaders there prefer instead the term *strategic partners*. Their idea is to share best practices and encourage leadership development.[10] Some local partners may become campuses of North Point, which means they link themselves to the other campuses financially and organizationally. The strategic partners beyond Atlanta are independent congregations who share North Point's philosophy and are licensed to use North Point video sermons and other materials.

For New Life Community Church in Chicago, where Mark Jobe is pastor, six of its first ten campuses were mergers, which they call Restarts. Three were congregations that had been established over one hundred years previously. New Life is now training other churches, especially urban ones, in how the legacy of faith can be powerfully honored and given fresh passion through a Restart.[11]

Other churches actively solicit merger partners but do so regionally. For example, Eagle Brook Church, led by Bob Merritt, is looking for partners in the greater Minneapolis–Saint Paul area as it seeks to establish a ring of campuses around the entire metroplex.[12] Likewise The Chapel in Grayslake, Illinois, is seeking to build a hub of merger churches around the suburban-rural outer edge of Chicago.

Bay Area Fellowship in Corpus Christi, Texas, where Bil Cornelius is pastor, invites church planters in particular to merge their congregations with Bay Area Fellowship as a way of spurring each other on to greater missional focus.[13]

Granted, megachurches like Mars Hill, North Point, Eagle Brook, The Chapel, and Bay Area Fellowship represent less than 1 percent of North America's churches. Yet the innovations they introduce and popularize often have a ripple effect across churches of all sizes. "One factor in the spread of new ideas is what *Diffusion of Innovations* author Everett Rogers calls their observability,"[14] says Dave Travis, managing director of Leadership Network and coauthor of *Beyond Megachurch Myths*.[15] "Some people hear an idea, grasp it, internalize it, and immediately start implementing it, but an even greater number of people have to *see* it first to understand. Once they see the model and its favorable results, they may decide that it has merit and value for them. Larger churches, due to their visibility and influence, often platform new models of ministry, which are then spread and adapted across the social ecosystem of smaller churches."

Clearly, larger churches are blazing a trail of extending their reach and multiplying their impact through intentional merger strategies that many other churches will follow in the days ahead.

Why Mergers in the Past Often Failed

How are today's mergers different from those of yesteryear? They represent two completely different paradigms that we might call "new math" and "old math" of church mergers. Old math mergers were more survival driven, whereas today's mergers are more mission driven. Also old math mergers worked toward equality between the merging churches where today's focus is on aligning with the stronger church culture.

> *Old math mergers were more survival driven, whereas today's mergers are more mission driven.*

First, the old math of mergers was too often 1 + 1 = 1. The combination rarely worked to produce a vibrant, healthy, larger, or growing church. As veteran church consultant Lyle Schaller explains, the newly merged church typically shrinks to the approximate size of the larger of the two former congregations because no one has made any effort to alter the congregational culture. Members were more comfortable in the smaller size environment they knew before the merger, so they keep dropping away until the culture goes back to what it was. As a result, the typical merger of two smaller no-growth churches "has had a spectacularly poor record in attracting new members," he says.[16] This situation commonly occurs, according to Schaller, even when there's a good cultural fit between the congregations.

One reason for failure is that the old approach often embodied little more than a goal to survive. It was seen as a way of preserving as much as possible. It was not portrayed as a vehicle that could bring significant change. These "intensive care" mergers of two struggling churches were a last-gasp effort to stay alive but often ended with both going down together, such as in the equation $1 + 1 = 0$.

At best, merging was wrongly perceived as a way of making the church work better. Two struggling churches (or sometimes three) would take what they thought were the best elements from each of them and combine them into a merged congregation.

By contrast, today's successful mergers tend to be missional in focus with one church embracing the vision and strategy of the other church. The new math has a synergistic effect. The merge represents far more than an action taken to survive. Such churches are motivated by a strong, future-oriented sense of mission and expanded outreach rather than by a desire for institutional survival. They are often preceded by three exploratory questions to determine a merger possibility:

- Could we accomplish more together than separately?
- Would our community be better served?
- Could the kingdom of God be further extended by our merger?

Those questions represent the heart of a mission-driven merger. Though many of today's merger conversations begin when a struggling congregation acknowledges its precarious circumstance, it is not only motivated by survival but by the dream of a renewed or greater mission.

What can make the difference needed for success? Schaller says, "The critical component is a minister who is an effective transformational leader and possesses the skills, including the essential people skills, necessary to create a new worshipping community with a new congregational culture, a strong future orientation, a new set of operational goals, a new sense of unity and a new approach to winning a new generation of members."[17]

What's the most practical way for that to happen? The best merger success stories, according to Schaller, tend to be when three congregations—rather than the more common pattern of two—come together to create a new congregation that constructs a new building at a new site under a new name with the strong leadership of a new minister who is comfortable and competent in the role of being the pastor of a middle-sized (or large) congregation. Further, within a few years at least one-half of the governing board is composed of people who have joined since the merger and who want to be part of a large and numerically growing congregation.[18]

The best merger success stories, according to Schaller, tend to be when three congregations . . . come together to create a new congregation.

Indeed, that is happening. As Gary Shockley, executive director for new church starts in the United Methodist Church, told us, "One of the strategies we see working in our denomination is the 'vital merger' where two or more churches sell all their assets, relocate, get a church planter assigned to them and begin anew."

Second, church mergers today are different from those in the past in that at least one of the partners is healthy and vital. Usually the healthy and more vital partner is larger in attendance. Sometimes it's the same size as the church merging with it. On rare occasions it's smaller than the church merging with it.

Whatever the size comparison, mergers are rarely a fifty-fifty deal of equals coming together. One church typically takes the lead role, expanding its culture of growing, replicating, and multiplying. If the merger is successful, far more

Mergers are rarely a fifty-fifty deal of equals coming together.

than survival happens for the joining church in the years after the merger. Instead it's a clear gain. The joining church is revitalized as the lead church's healthy momentum continues with evidence of more changed lives, more conversions, more baptisms, and more signs of spiritual vitality.

A Dream of Greater Kingdom Ministry

A Colorado pastor told us how he had become the pastor of a small church that had met in a school for five years without effective growth. "Members were tired of trying to push the boulder up a hill with only limited success in all areas," he said. "They were definitely exhausted by setting up in a school every week for five years."

Elders in the congregation raised the topic of a potential merger, looking for the right circumstances. They found a growing, "unleashing" kind of church in Bear Valley Church and asked their pastor to approach its leaders.

By all counts, the merger went well. The pastor told us,

It was successful because both churches understood there is no such thing as an even-steven merger. One church must assume the other. We helped our folks see that what mattered most wasn't "the church of us" but "the church of Jesus." In other words, we rightfully portrayed this as a way to maximize our Kingdom impact—just the opposite of a corporate take-over. We further helped those in the joining church transition into the larger body by forming a large Sunday adult class, which helped maintain their close fellowship. Eventually most of the new people assimilated into the ministries of the lead church.

The joining church gave away its old facility to another church that is still using it to this day. "We merged because we could accomplish more kingdom ministry together than by remaining separate," he concluded.

This pastor personally modeled a humility and kingdom mind-set by joining the lead church in an assistant pastor role with only occasional preaching opportunities. Other than wishing he had asked to preach a little more often, he says he has no regrets about the merger.

This is the kind of story we suspect we'll all hear more about in the years to come.

2

FOUR MODELS FOR HEALTHY MERGERS

Though all mergers involve a lead church and a joining church, not all mergers are the same or look alike. They vary by many factors including size, whether they change or keep their name, and whether they remain single site or become multisite as part of the merger.

Perhaps the most important way mergers differ is in the model they follow. As Chapter One explained, not everyone uses the term *merger*. The word *merger* contains a lot of emotional baggage, mostly negative. We'd like to introduce a set of family-related terms to describe the various ways churches can merge. Here's a quick summary, followed by a description, profile, and pros and cons of each one:

- *Rebirth mergers:* A struggling or dying church that gets a second life by being restarted under a stronger, vibrant, and typically larger church
- *Adoption mergers:* A stable or stuck church that is integrated under the vision of a stronger, vibrant, and typically larger church
- *Marriage mergers:* Two churches, both strong or growing, that realign with each other under a united vision and new leadership configuration
- *ICU (intensive care unit) mergers:* Two churches that know they're in trouble and try to turn around their critical situation but are more survival driven and often fail

How do these terms relate to each other? Each has distinctive elements but they're not exclusive from each other. On one spectrum, an adoption merger is in the middle between a rebirth merger and a marriage merger. An ICU merger is usually a merger of two near equals, both on life support. These are more reflective of the typical failed mergers of the past.

Every church merger has potential gains and losses. There are no guarantees.

Every church merger has potential gains and losses. There are no guarantees. There are pros and cons to be prayerfully evaluated with every kind.

The potential gains are dramatic. Church mergers can multiply church impact, increase outreach, produce synergistic ministries, revitalize churches, restore facilities, serve communities better, and revive new hope for the future. These potential gains are driving the church merger movement today.

The potential losses can be equally dramatic. Churches can lose their name and facilities. The pastor, staff, and favorite ministry may not survive the transition. Not all members stay, and some good friends may leave. What is most painful is the potential for the heritage and identity of a church to get lost in the merger process. These are all very real and very difficult possible outcomes of a church merger.

In the following section we share examples of each merger model followed by commentary describing the pros and cons of that particular model.

Rebirth Mergers

Rebirth mergers occur when a struggling or dying church gets a second life by being restarted under a stronger, vibrant, and typically larger church. In our view the majority of mergers are rebirths, even though they might not use that term. Further, rebirths may occur with some or all of the previous congregation becoming part of the new entity.

Example

In fall 1917 a small group of residents in Fairbanks, Louisiana, gathered in a one-room schoolhouse built of rough lumber to organize a church. Three years later a local business built a small structure to be used as a community building. Over time it came to be known as Union Church as different denominations took turns on Sundays leading church services in it. In more recent times it became Fairbanks Baptist Church. Members bought additional property, built buildings, and called various pastors over the years. Attendance peaked in the 1990s at around three hundred.

In March 2011, after Fairbanks Baptist Church had declined for years, its leadership called a church conference with about twenty-five people present. They discussed where they would be in a year. They decided that they could be proactive about their church or they could let circumstances determine the church's future. After discussion they voted unanimously to ask First Baptist Church of West Monroe, Louisiana, to enter into what they called a "partnership" with them.

A feasibility committee was created composed of representatives from both churches. Together they recommended a plan in which Fairbanks Baptist Church would dissolve and rebirth as a multisite campus of First Baptist Church of West Monroe, Louisiana.

The recommendation was approved 28:1 by a congregational vote of Fairbanks Baptist Church in August 2011. The church was immediately dissolved, the assets were deeded over to First Baptist Church of West Monroe, and the plans for relaunching the campus began. During the renovations, the members began attending the First Baptist Church of West Monroe and were part of the launch core team of the new First West Fairbanks campus in January 2012.

The dying church of twenty-five had been rebirthed with over one hundred people—and a new chapter began, one filled with hope.

Pros and Cons

Candidates for a rebirth merger can come from the nearly quarter of a million Protestant churches across the United States that are struggling, in decline, or dying. The majority of these churches have fewer than two hundred people in attendance, a good portion fewer than seventy-five people weekly.[1] Too many of them are more focused on maintenance or survival than on transforming their communities. Roughly three thousand of these churches (1 percent of all churches in America) will close their doors permanently nationwide in the next twelve months.

These dying congregations have empty facilities in need of repair that could be infused with the life-giving DNA of a healthy, growing church. Their empty seats could be filled again. The dream of the founders could be resurrected and extended in a merger with an effective, successful church. They can celebrate the past but not be stuck there. All of these congregations started with hope and a vision. Today, most of them are discouraged and barely hanging on.

Like Fairbanks Baptist Church in Louisiana, most of these churches possess land and facilities that are currently underutilized. Like Fairbanks Baptist, they can be reborn and find a second life through merging with a dynamic and vibrant church. They don't need renewal; they need a rebirth.

The most successful rebirths occur when the joining church is smart enough or desperate enough to be willing to

The decision to merge usually does not happen until church leaders conclude that the pain of not changing is greater than the pain of changing.

relinquish everything to the lead church—its name, facilities, staff, ministries, and glorious past—all in exchange for a second life. The decision to merge usually does not happen until church leaders conclude that the pain of not changing is greater than the pain of changing. Their attitude becomes, "If we do nothing, we die. If we merge, we live." Then the odds increase for a successful merger with a strong church.

Most church mergers include a name change. Leadership Network's research confirmed that the majority of mergers involve a name change, usually by the joining church. Sometimes both churches come up with a new name all together.

Sometimes, because of stewardship or strategic reasons, a merger will result in a sale of the joining church's building. Leadership Network's research also revealed that half of all mergers involving two facilities become multisite, a fourth sell one of the facilities, and a fourth use the second facility for other purposes such as a ministry base or offices.

Even if a church loses its building through a merger it does not have to lose its heritage or give up its identity. Though it may be necessary to sell the facilities, wise church leaders recognize that a church's heritage and identity are built around a place. A lot of blood, sweat, and tears of the joining congregation have been invested in their facility. There is a lot of emotion tied to that place. People poured not only their resources but also their lives into the building that is now being sold. Many found Christ in that building, many were baptized or dedicated their children to God there; some were married in that place. Savvy church leaders are sensitive to the grieving process that comes with the loss of that building. They learn the history, culture, and identity of the joining church and discover the healthy traits to build on in creating a new future together.

Mergers are not really the beginning of a new work in the community but are more of a rebuilding on the good work that had begun years ago, sometimes decades earlier. Instead of erasing the past, smart church leaders bless the past and communicate how the merger carries on the mission of the former days. Pastor Mark Jobe says it well in the Restart video, available online, that explains the merger strategy of New Life Community Church in Chicago: "God has been at work in that neighborhood long before we came on the scene. God has been working sometimes a hundred years before we ever got there and it's on our hearts to say, 'Can we cooperate with what God is already doing (in this neighborhood)?'"[2] Healthy rebirth mergers don't reject or erase the identity of the joining church but incorporate it into the new identity.

Unfortunately, it is easier to give birth than produce a resurrection. Most of these declining churches would rather hang on to their control rather than turn the wheel over to someone who knows how to steer it out of a death spiral. Some will die this year—on average 1 percent of the churches in your community will be gone by this time next year. Most will hang on for years but will make little difference, if any, in their community. Their focus is on surviving and preserving rather than embracing a new vision for the future with a stronger church. They would rather have a "partnership" with a stronger church that allows them to survive, but not really have to change. These churches don't need a partner; they need to be absorbed by a strong church, which is what the rebirth idea conveys.

Their focus is on surviving and preserving rather than embracing a new vision for the future with a stronger church.

Rebirth mergers can be wonderful win-win for both churches when the joining church correctly understands its current reality, but it can be a huge drain of time, energy, and resources when the declining church doesn't fully embrace the future under new leadership of the lead church.

The temptation for a lead church is to pour a lot of time and resources into a declining church that has no intention of changing. Like a lifeguard trying to rescue a man from drowning, they both can be dragged under by the drowning man struggling to keep his head above water.

Jesus warned about people who pour new wine in old wineskins. "If they do, the new wine will burst the skins. The wine will run out, and the wineskins will be destroyed. No, new wine must be poured into new wineskins" (Luke 5:37–38).

An Atlanta pastor who went through a merger summarizes well the challenge and opportunity of rebirth mergers: "When understood as a vehicle to change rather than to conserve, to displace rather than protect, to shatter the old rather than restore, mergers can be a powerful tool for advancing the congregation's God-given mission."[3]

Adoption Model

Adoption mergers are typically stable or stuck churches that integrate under the vision of a stronger, vibrant, and typically larger church.

Example

It took a lot of hard work and prayer for a core group of families to keep Grace Baptist Church in Bountiful, Utah, viable through the years. So when the chance came to merge with what is likely Utah's largest-attendance Protestant church, Washington Heights, twenty miles north in Ogden, the faithful at Grace Baptist were both relieved and wary. But they explored the merger idea because, as one of the members told a local newspaper, "We just felt like God gave us an opportunity to blend these two church families together and that together we could do a lot more for the community."[4]

The two churches, sister congregations in the Conservative Baptist Association, voted overwhelmingly in 2010 to join forces. The congregation in Bountiful, renamed as Bountiful Heights, became a second site of Washington Heights Church.

Handling administrative tasks in Ogden means the pastors are freed for ministry when they are in Bountiful, says senior pastor Roy Gruber, who now keeps an office at both campuses. "It really allows us to focus on ministry and the people," he says.

Since the alliance, attendance is up at Bountiful Heights from seventy to over two hundred, mostly from word-of-mouth advertising about the changes under way, Gruber says. A children's ministry is rolling, and ten to fifteen youths regularly gather on Sunday nights now. "That's a large part of what we're about," he says. "We do want to share our good news with our community, but mostly that happens life to life and people inviting their friends and neighbors."

Bountiful Heights has neither the parking nor the building to grow as large as Washington Heights, which exceeds two thousand people on a typical Sunday. "We're great with that," Gruber says. "It isn't about how many folks we can get in one location. It's about reaching out as much as we can. This merger was a real opportunity for like-minded churches to work together and do good for the community."[5]

Pros and Cons

If limited to the terms in our book, most churches would describe their merger as an adoption, but in our view most are rebirths. Adoption mergers are not for desperate churches in danger of immediate extinction but more for stable or stuck churches who embrace the synergistic benefit of joining a stronger church. They recognize that their church's mission will be better fulfilled by submitting their name, ministries, and assets to a church that can multiply its impact beyond what it could do by remaining solo. Though the adopted church turns over everything to the lead church, it usually brings something to the table in addition to a congregation of people: facilities, staff, and ministry programs that are often integrated into the lead church's overall strategy. Like an adopted child, they take on a

new name and relation-
ship, but they also add a
dimension to their new
parent that enhances
the whole family.

> *Most churches would describe their merger as an adoption, but in our view most are rebirths.*

As in rebirth merg-
ers there is usually a name change—and the potential loss of
facilities, staff, ministries, members, and friends, but it does not
have to be at the expense of losing the church's heritage and
identity.

There is also the potential for added disappointment,
change resistance, and conflict postmerger because adopted
churches, as they approach a merger, don't feel as desperate as
rebirth churches. Therefore they often don't feel the need to
embrace the change as strongly.

Marriage Merger

Marriage mergers occur when two churches, both of which
are strong or growing, realign with each other under a
united vision and new leadership configuration. Marriage
mergers in churches are much like a marriage of husband
and wife: people entering marriages bring both strengths and
liabilities. And like a lot of human marriages, churches coming together may have some difficulties, but they can work
through them.

Example

Unlike most human marriages, church marriage mergers often
involve two churches at different stages in their life cycles. One
marriage merger that has made the headlines of late for its semi-
celebrity pastors and its adjustments to "married" life began
after one pastor died of a heart attack at age seventy-six. It is
never an easy task to find a successor for a much-loved, highly

successful founding pastor, especially one who was at the helm of his church for twenty-eight years. Coral Ridge Presbyterian Church, Fort Lauderdale, Florida, was no exception as D. James Kennedy, its nationally known pastor, passed away and a pastoral search began.

After a fourteen-month search a candidate was named: Pastor Tullian Tchividjian, age thirty-six, and grandson of Billy Graham. However, he had agreed to consider the position only if New City Church, twelve miles away, which he had founded five years earlier, could merge with Coral Ridge as part of the process.

The two churches formally came together on Easter 2009, bringing changes to the leadership and worship style. "We knew that was going to be in some ways a clash of culture," Tullian says. "We knew that blending two families is never an easy task, and it wasn't." According to Tullian there was a small but very vocal group in the church "who didn't want anything to change and who were questioning all the decisions that we were making from the moment we got there. It really got ugly pretty quickly." The group of dissidents lost a congregational vote to undo the merger and left to form a different church. Yet by the one-year mark membership, attendance, and donations were all up from when Tullian came, and continued to grow. Some of the people who left also returned.

As this book goes to press, Coral Ridge continues to experience many signs of renewed vitality and ongoing growth, though at the initial cost of what Tullian describes as "the most painful year of my life." This unfortunate reality highlights the dangers of some mergers. But not all marriage mergers have new relatives that squabble so vocally! In Chapters One and Thirteen we describe another marriage merger named Redemption Church, in which two churches came together without the same level of dissention, bringing a lot of strengths and resources to the table, even though they, too, were at different life stages.[6]

Pros and Cons

Marriage mergers have the greatest potential gains of all church mergers because both churches bring mutually beneficial, complementary strengths and assets to the merger. They create the greatest synergy because both churches are typically healthy, strong, and united under a compelling mission and vision that they have created together. Marriage mergers can also be a vehicle for a seamless senior pastor succession strategy, as described in Chapter Three.

The greatest challenge in marriage mergers is when there is a cosharing of the senior pastor role—such as the senior pastors from each church becoming co-pastors. It is an unusual senior pastor who is willing to share or submit the leadership role to another. Two coleaders under one roof usually produce some explosive outcomes!

Marriage mergers are rather rare because few mergers occur between churches where both bring a significant number of complimentary strengths. Many mergers are described to the respective churches as a marriage merger but in reality are more of a rebirth or an adoption merger. Using marriage merger language can raise the egalitarian expectations in the joining congregation when in fact it is more of a hierarchal relationship. It can later feel like a bait-and-switch scenario, which often causes a lot of resentment and disappointment postmerger.

ICU Merger

The least successful type of merger comes from the joining of two or more churches that feel like they're in an intensive care unit. Typically they've each faced many years of decline and have tried one or more interventions to start a new wave of life, none with success.

Example

In her book, *Can Our Church Live?*, Alban Institute consultant Alice Mann describes two Massachusetts congregations that "beat the odds and gained significant vitality from the consolidation process."[7] The process involved a new pastor who was an entrepreneurial leader and change agent. She won the people's loyalty by listening, caring, and taking steps of faith with them. Through a multiyear series of intentional developments, the merged church took a new name and developed a whole new identity. The slow decline of both congregations was reversed, and the resulting new congregation entered a new era with hope and promise.

Pros and Cons

Joining together may buy time and hope in order to figure out how to turn around the decline and make the changes necessary to experience health and growth. In rare cases, as in the previous example, ICU mergers do begin gaining ground again, especially if they get a new unified vision, new growth-minded leader, new location, and a new name. ICU units always contain hope that the patient will get better, and on occasion ICU mergers do make it.

On the con side, this kind of church merger represents the majority of failed mergers of the past because they are often unwilling or unable to change. It is a rare church leader who can lead these churches to turnaround. Church consultant Gary McIntosh concludes that only about 5 percent of pastors are turnaround leaders.[8] Thom Rainer, who has done years of research for the Southern Baptist Convention, notes that "there are not enough turnaround pastors to lead even one-third of America's" churches in need of turnaround.[9]

ICU mergers typically fail because they are like two drowning men clinging to each other, neither letting the other take charge.

ICU mergers typically fail because they are like two drowning men clinging to each other, neither letting the other take charge.

They end up taking each other down. Instead of a recovery, they both end up dying side by side in the hospice ward. They often have good intentions, but without making other changes that infuse life, they are at best prolonging the inevitable.

Alice Mann's book *Can Our Church Live?* is subtitled *Redeveloping Congregations in Decline* because that is her focus. In it she strongly discourages what we're calling the ICU merger approach in which all parties are in the later steps of decline.

"Why doesn't the consolidation of several weak congregations produce one strong one?" she asks. Partly because it encourages people to focus inward, she says:

> Often, merged congregations [of this type] spend a lot of time deciding whose candlesticks will be used at Christmas and not much energy asking: "Who lives in this community today, and how could we reach them?" The inability to answer that question creatively is part of the reason membership is declining in the first place. Even if members decide to take a new look at identity and purpose, the work becomes tougher, since two or more narratives are involved.[10]

Realistic Hope

All mergers, like all human beings, are messy and complicated with no guarantees. Every church merger has a unique pathway. There is no one-size-fits-all formula they all follow, yet all will wrestle with the same basic issues. How they address and manage those issues will vary from church to church but the first step is to understand what kind of merger is being considered and the pros and cons that come with each type of merger.

3

MISSIONAL, MULTISITE, MULTIETHNIC, AND OTHER MERGER MOTIVES

The starting point for successful church mergers today is a strong motivation beyond just survival or even a desire for local church unity. Mergers have the best chance of success when they are unified around a clear, biblically based mission and share a common theology and faith practice. Survival and unity are not strong enough motivators for successful mergers, but successful mergers do generate unity and revitalize struggling churches. The Apostle Paul captures the power of unity around a common purpose when he exhorted the church at Philippi to be "like-minded . . . being one in spirit and purpose" (Phil. 2:4).

Of the dozens of interviews we conducted for this book, the story of a 2005 merger of two small churches in rural Ohio has to rank as the messiest mix of motives that we have heard. Yet it ended positively. "We serve a God of redemption who certainly redeemed this situation," said Tim Broughton, who shifted from worship pastor to lead pastor in the middle of the merger. "And perhaps it's not ironic that the resulting church is named New Hope."

The drama brought together New Hope Church, then a fledgling congregation desperate for a facility, with a church that possessed a building but couldn't agree on a response to its declining numbers. Although they were both from the same denomination, each had a hard time seeing the other in a positive light. Today, looking back, each would probably say it wasn't healthy enough to merge, as was demonstrated by the drama that was played out in the editorial column of the local newspapers as people who had left the older congregation went public with their case.

It took a long and painful year from first discussion until the two churches landed in a better place as one merged church with clarified vision and forward momentum. The older of the two (which also had the building) became the joining church. It had once been a strong congregation with involvement from many leading families in the community, but in more recent years attendance had declined. Church leaders brought in a younger pastor who tried to move it to be more culturally relevant in worship and style, but attendance only shrunk further. The remaining attendees became discouraged.

That church's young pastor became aware of New Hope Church, then meeting in a high school, as a model of what he was trying to do. He started to build a relationship between New Hope's leaders and his own. He led the forty remaining attendees of his church to make the near-unanimous decision to merge with New Hope. Then he resigned, knowing that New Hope didn't have a role for him. Immediately, twenty-five to thirty longtime members who had left his church in recent years came back and opposed the merger. "How can you make those decisions?" they asked those who had remained.

Meanwhile the congregation at New Hope likewise entered the merger with some unhealthy expectations. Some wrongly saw the move into a building as a chance for them to back off from being so involved now that they wouldn't have to do weekly setup and would have more people to help. Others viewed their potential suitor more as a financial feeder than as a true partner in ministry.

Both churches had inappropriate or inaccurate motives to work through. "We wish we had used a third-party consultant who didn't have a dog in the fight," says New Hope's Tim Broughton.

Yet God walked them through the messiness as all parties got to know each other and people refocused on cooperating with

God to see lives changed through the gospel. "When people see the gospel preached and working, there is no more argument," Tim says. "Over the months everyone saw that we're following the same mission as when the older congregation built their twenty-year-old building. Trust grew. Some people who had opposed the merger came back and rejoined us."

At the time of the merger combined attendance was 140. Five years later it was over two hundred. The environment of the church grows healthier with each passing year. "The most recent months have clearly been the most fun either of us has had," Tim says, referring to the sense of joy his congregation is now experiencing.

Wrong Motives

Church mergers happen due to a number of motives, wrong and right, immature and healthy. Improper motives include the following:

- *Preservation:* Viewing the merger as a "marriage" designed to perpetuate the current church culture with more hope in preserving the past than in developing a new future. However, if a church is not willing to really change, a new name and a few more resources won't turn the church around.

- *Denial:* Using the merger as a tactic to avoid or distract from addressing deeper problems or systemic issues. It's like launching a building program instead of dealing with something that is badly broken.

- *Personal gain:* Using the merger as a strategy to create a co-pastor or multistaff role as job security for a church leader or to help out a friend whose church is in trouble. Perhaps an underpaid pastor wants a more steady salary or someone wants to provide a retirement or golden parachute exit strategy for an aging senior pastor. These are hardly noble reasons to base a merger on, much less do they provide a strong-enough foundation to do so.

- *Financial motivation only:* Using the merger as a strategy to raise cash for an endowment or for deferred maintenance needs; likewise, not caring about the people, just wanting their assets such as their facility, location, or the prestige of their heritage.

- *Personal glory:* Desiring to experiment in order to make news, or perhaps to create an attention-gaining strategy for a pastor with a big ego.

We wouldn't make this list of unfortunate motives if we hadn't heard stories of most of these things happening. Scripture abounds with accounts of how God made good with any number of messes, selfish people, and even downright evil doings, but let us underscore that healthy mergers work best when they're birthed from healthy motives. Chapter Ten is devoted to how churches discern and hear God's leading. Obeying God fully is a non-negotiable, and shady means are never a wise path to a God-honoring end.

Healthy mergers work best when they're birthed from healthy motives. . . . Shady means are never a wise path to a God-honoring end.

Temptations Good and Bad

Some circumstances are not questionable in themselves, but they can lead to inappropriate motives or to mergers laced with distrust. Here are the two most common that we encounter.

Valuable Property

The denomination Warren is part of was initially based in the Times Square area of New York City. Today the church building is a restaurant, and Warren recently had pizza there. The facility that at one time hosted his denomination's flagship church has only a wall plaque newspaper clipping about the era when it focused on nourishment for the soul rather than serving food for the body.

That situation is not unique as each year some three thousand Protestant churches in the United States close their doors forever. In fact, Warren has an entire collection of photos he's taken of former church buildings. The majority have become residences or restaurants. Others have become businesses and breweries.

Churches represent a lot of valuable real estate, often worth millions, sometimes ideally located, and usually zoned with favorable conditions that the surrounding community would no longer grant today. Not only do real estate developers see great potential in these sites but faith groups do too, such as would-be suitors for a church merger. Although good organizations exist for churches that decide to permanently close, helping them distribute their assets to a new generation of churches,[1] merger talks may also begin directly between two churches or perhaps through a denominational mediary.

The key is for the church that might acquire such valuable properties to keep right priorities and pure motives. As our friend Craig Groeschel, founding pastor or Oklahoma-based LifeChurch.tv and writer of this book's Foreword, says:

> If the stronger church doesn't believe it can truly help the weaker one and serve them with integrity, the stronger church should not move forward. I've seen stronger church leaders make unrealistic promises all in an attempt to get a building from a struggling church. Remember—it is not all about buildings! It is all about people! At LifeChurch.tv, we have declined far more merger possibilities than we've accepted because we didn't think it would be in the best interest of the other church.[2]

Denominational Pressure

A good number of mergers are within the same denominational family, such as two Evangelical Lutheran Church in America congregations coming together. Others come from similar church families, such as two independent Baptists merging or a Presbyterian Church in America church merging with one affiliated with the Evangelical Presbyterian Church. Or perhaps two nondenominational churches with similar doctrines and styles will merge. But are churches pressured to merge by denominational authorities, even if the likelihood of success is not strong?

Decades ago when several US denominations were merging and the ecumenical movement was still in its idealism stage, there was no doubt more pressure on even unwilling churches to merge, causing the high failure rate that Lyle Schaller and others observed in their writings between the 1900s and about the 1960s.

Today hierarchical denominations still have the same power to require a merger but they tend to exercise it more collaboratively with the involved churches. Typical is the observation Jorge Acevedo expressed to us in our interviews:

> My experience in Cape Coral, Florida, and what I hear from fellow United Methodist leaders, is that more pastors of prevailing United Methodist churches are taking the initiative to begin conversation with lagging and failing congregations in their community. They see the potential of "transfer of DNA" from a stronger church to a declining church. Strategically, this transfer happens through leadership with clear mission, vision, values, strategy and structures as well as mutually agreed upon policies and guidelines. In our experience of adopting two declining churches, in one situation I initiated the conversation with the appropriate hierarchy and in the other my District Superintendent initiated the conversation.

If Jorge's experience is typical, then denominational mergers are moving in a direction to allow trust to build with both congregations, who can then reach goal ownership and adjustments within areas of negotiable issues. The temptation to railroad a takeover is still present but the process rarely has to go that direction. Nondictated, mutually desired mergers always have a higher likelihood of success.

> *Nondictated . . . mergers always have a higher likelihood of success.*

Potentially Healthy Motives

There are at least six frequently found reasons why churches might want to merge. Each can have a healthy impetus behind it.

Mission-Driven Mind-Sets

Most successful mergers today are mission-driven rather than the survival-driven mergers of the past. They occur when churches discern that their synergy could lead to a greater impact for the kingdom of God. The synergistic benefit of joining with like-minded churches on a similar mission affirms the wisdom of Solomon, who said, "Two are better than one, for they have a good return for their work" (Eccles. 4:9). Some are struggling churches but many are not. Some are made possible because of a multisite strategy but most are not.

As we explained in Chapter One, the old model was for two or three struggling churches to merge together, but unfortunately that typically resulted in a new church that still struggled. A year or two after the merger, total attendance had settled back to the level of the larger church, and it wasn't growing. The old model was 1 + 1 = 0 or maybe 1 + 1 = 1, but the new model often results in 1 + 1 = 3 or more.

Economic-Driven Pressures

It is not difficult to find churches that are experiencing serious financial challenges, from an extreme of property foreclosure to more common situations of selling properties or downsizing ministry and cutting back their pastor hours due to lack of funding. Church foreclosures, virtually unheard of in the United States before the Great Recession of 2008, have recently increased in number. According to a *Wall Street Journal* report nearly two hundred churches have had their properties foreclosed on by banks in 2008, 2009, and 2010, up from only eight foreclosures in the two years prior to that and none in the previous decade.[3]

Church financial woes are not limited to the recent economic downturn. One recent study found that the percentage of congregations reporting some or serious financial difficulty more than doubled to nearly 20 percent since about 2000. From 2000 to 2008—before the recession's toll was felt— congregations reporting "excellent financial health" had dropped from 31 percent to 19 percent. They dropped further to 14 percent in 2010. The recession only exacerbated their economic situations, according to survey compiler David Roozen, director of The Hartford Institute for Religion Research.[4]

Certain financial challenges are almost predictable, with or without a recession. Many churches hit a stage in their life cycle when they cannot go forward without a totally new start. The early days of most churches are marked by growth, conversions, young families, and different forms of innovation such as a fresh worship style or a new way of serving the surrounding community in Jesus's name. Over the years, a triple whammy factor can develop: the average age within the congregation becomes ten to twenty years older than that of the people in the surrounding community, making it harder to attract new people; the pastor tends to be more senior in age, again adding challenge to efforts to attract younger newcomers; and likewise, the church facility grows older and needier in terms of costly maintenance, which adds more burden to the existing members.

A church like this can slowly lose its appeal to newcomers, especially younger generations, causing the congregation to decline further in attendance and to struggle further in its ability to go forward. As the cycle spins downward, corporate discouragement often sets in. Eventually a crisis—sometimes as simple as the need for major facility repair or the retiring of the current pastor—triggers a church to prayerfully consider, "Maybe we should merge with a like-minded, healthy congregation that's doing the job we want to be doing."

We believe an increasing number of churches are opting for mergers due to the economic recession of recent years that has forced many churches to reassess their long-term viability. Under prosperous times many churches were propped up by artificial life support that no longer exists for many of them. Many church leaders are concluding that a merger may be a way to have a "second life" instead of closing the doors of the church permanently or limping along into a doubtful future. Of the roughly three hundred thousand Protestant churches in the United States, most church experts say that nearly 80 percent are stuck, struggling, or in decline.

Think about the scope of those numbers: 80 percent of three hundred thousand churches means nearly a quarter million churches across the country have room in their facilities to fill with vibrant ministry. Meanwhile, there are a few thousand dynamic, growing, vibrant churches in desperate need of facilities. Can you imagine the win-win here? Certainly some of these churches can find new growth and vitality on their own as they pursue Jesus's mission to "seek and save what was lost" (Luke 19:10). There will also be many who are willing to join with a vibrant church in the days ahead. That means many are strong candidates for a merger.

Multisite-Driven Momentum

The congregation known today as Sunrise Church started in 1956, grew steadily, going from one to several weekend services, and relocated several times in and around Rialto, California. Today it is one church in multiple sites, each location becoming part of the church under different circumstances.

The first offsite campus came in 1996 through a merger and was the result of a dying congregation in the same denomination that approached Sunrise for assistance. The church is now a Sunrise Church campus and enjoys the benefits of being part of a much larger church beyond its campus.

The second offsite location was the result of two congregations a mile apart that had discussed a merger among themselves prior to becoming a part of the Sunrise Church family. One of the churches approached Sunrise to merge and then the other church wanted to merge as well. The process was first a merger of these two churches with Sunrise Church, and then combining them to become the Sunrise Church Ontario campus.

The third offsite location was a Grace Brethren Church, which was composed of a very small group of people. They worked very hard to grow and reach out to the community in middle Rialto for many years with little long-term result. After a few church makeovers the pastor approached Sunrise Church seeking guidance. The merger was successful, and it is now a fourth Sunrise campus although still in the Grace Brethren denomination of churches—a campus with dual-denomination membership.

Sunrise East Valley (thirty-five miles way) was started in part to provide a campus for church members who moved east of the Sunrise Church Rialto campus and to reach out to the unchurched in the East Valley. It has been from inception a Sunrise campus rather than a separate new church.

In every case Sunrise Church staff and key ministry coordinators provided the following:

- Training for the pastoral staff and ministry counterparts
- Curriculum for use in the teaching ministries
- Outreach strategies
- A spiritual growth process
- Aspects of intentionality to promote multiethnic, multicultural ministry

According to staff pastor Art Valadez, who is in charge of the church's sites and its church planting, "Multisite has worked well for us for many reasons. It has enabled us to reach out to people far beyond our immediate community and city. It has also provided local congregations within our church for those who move out of Rialto and still want to be a part of Sunrise Church. Multisite has been a great tool for discipleship on many levels and has challenged us to stretch beyond our comfort zone in developing new leaders. Even though all our buildings are now built and paid for and we enjoy a beautiful, newer 2,000-seat worship center, multisite helps us to partner with others and continue a healthy outward focus."

Sunrise Church is not alone. The multisite church movement has definitely contributed to the recent rise in church mergers. According to Leadership Network research, one out of three multisite campuses are the result of a church merger.[5]

According to Leadership Network research, one out of three multisite campuses are the result of a church merger.

And the multisite phenomenon continues to grow rapidly. Every week over five million people attend one of three thousand plus multisite campuses across the United States. There are more multisite churches than megachurches. The majority of multisite churches have two or three campuses with an average weekend attendance of thirteen hundred. Multisite has truly become the "new normal" for healthy, growing, outreach-oriented churches and it is transforming the church scene across the nation.

The multisite movement began in the late 1990s as a bandage approach for megachurches that were out of room or limited by zoning restrictions. It quickly evolved into a growth strategy for healthy churches of all sizes and is increasingly becoming a revitalization strategy for stable, but stuck churches. It also is driving a new kind of church merger that is more mission and strategy driven than survival oriented.

Though the majority of church mergers today are not driven by multisite churches, multiplying through mergers is increasingly being seen as a fast track way to multisite when the conditions are right for a successful merger.

Crossing Denominational Lines   One of the most interesting aspects of these multisite mergers is how many cross denominational lines. One example is Granger Community Church, a United Methodist congregation in a suburb of South Bend, Indiana. Back in 2006 when it was meeting in one location, it had experienced twenty straight years of growth and its leaders were beginning to contemplate becoming a multisite church.

One of the towns that church leaders considered for their first offsite campus was Elkhart, Indiana. A church there, Saint Johns United Church of Christ, was diminishing in attendance and wondered about partnering with Granger but ultimately nothing happened as the majority of their leaders were not in favor of it.

"And honestly," says Granger executive pastor Tim Stevens, "we weren't ready yet either. We didn't know that at the time, but we had not yet embraced a multisite philosophy, we didn't have a point leader, and we hadn't identified a core of Granger families committed to that area."

By 2008, Granger had launched a site in Elkhart. It started at a movie theater and then moved to a larger site that began having financial troubles, prompting Granger to pray for a more stable and ideally more permanent location.

About that time, Saint Johns made the decision—after 122 years of ministry in Elkhart—to cease its weekly services and to find another church that could use its building. Their leaders approached Granger displaying, in the words of Tim Stevens, "an amazing heart of generosity." They did not want to see the property sold and used for retail. "They wanted to see a thriving local church having an impact in the community," Tim says.

Why Granger? Few at Saint Johns had even attended a service at Granger. Many of them weren't excited about the church's more contemporary style of ministry. But they had heard, over and over, of Granger's good work in the community feeding the hungry and helping the poor in Elkhart. They longed to see the same thing once again at St. Johns. In 2011, they officially transferred their property to Granger, worth $1.2 million. "That gift will enable us to host a 24/7/365 ministry outpost on the northeast side of Elkhart," Tim says.[6]

Chicken or Egg First?   Has multisite fueled mergers or have mergers fueled multisite? It works both ways but we see the first option as the larger motivator. It's like the interview Warren recently had with a reporter who pointed out the rise in available commercial real estate in a certain city and asked if it meant a bunch of churches would decide to open or relocate there. Warren explained that churches don't work that way in most cases. Most church plantings and expansions start with a leader who finds spiritual need among receptive people. Finding a good roof to put over their gatherings usually comes later.

But sometimes it does happen that available facilities lead to a church going multisite. Perhaps one church is struggling and is drawn to the fruitfulness God seems to be granting another church's ministry. Usually some kind of relationship is already present, either through a common denomination, network, or local ministerial fellowship. Discussions sometimes lead to the question, "How could we partner or collaborate together?" The answer, if the church isn't multisite already, sometimes is, "Well, it would work if we become multisite." Often as local church leaders share their lives with one another, trust develops, and the merger possibilities surface as an option to consider for serving their community in better ways.

The Leadership Network 2011 survey of church mergers documented many examples in which all these situations happened. The survey also revealed that multisite mergers have a higher rate of success and satisfaction than churches that merge into one location. Here is what the survey findings say about multisite mergers:

- The majority of multisite mergers are initiated by the joining church.
- The majority of multisite mergers occur within a thirty-minute driving distance of one another.
- The majority of multisite mergers involve a name change, usually of the joining church.
- The average length of the merger process beginning with an initial conversation to merger completion is seven months.
- Successful rated mergers report full integration within one year of the merger.
- Half of all mergers involving two facilities become multisite, a fourth sell a facility, and a fourth use the facility for other purposes.
- The majority of multisite mergers take a vote at both churches with an 80 to 100 percent "yes" response.[7]

Though most multisite churches do not start out to pursue mergers, some multisite churches have developed a church-merger strategy as part of their multisite strategy. In Chapter One we describe New Life Community Church in Chicago, which multiplies campuses through a merger strategy called Restart. New Life Community Church represents a small but growing number of multisite churches that are intentional in approaching other congregations about becoming one of their campuses. We know of another church in greater Chicago that learned that in any given year 1 percent of US Protestant churches close. "For me in the Chicago suburbs that is thirty-five to forty churches that may be in danger of shutting down this year," our pastor friend told us. "Finding them before that happens could be a huge Kingdom win."

Mostly from personal contacts, this church experienced five mergers between 2005 and 2011. Although this church is non-denominational, one merger church came from a denomination. When that congregation asked permission of their bishop, he released them saying, "That's now one less problem for me."

After the merger, the church began to grow. A founding member of the joining church was found crying after one of the services. They were tears of joy. "Pastor," she said, "This is the church I always knew we could be."

However, in the new era for mergers described in this book, the process more often starts with a growing church, one that embodies a big heart toward reaching new groups of people and an effectiveness at doing so. It is multisite already—or it's becoming multisite. It has often targeted an area for a new campus and is on the lookout for a potential meeting site. It's actively praying and asking around about possible site options, including churches that might benefit from a merger. Some of those discussions lead to mergers as an additional campus for the multisite church.

Succession-Driven Strategies

In summer 2006, senior pastor Gary Kinnaman announced to his church his plans to retire and to begin a nationwide search for a co-pastor who would become his successor. Gary had served Word of Grace in Mesa, Arizona, for twenty-five years and attendance had grown to over four thousand under his leadership, but its attendance had plateaued around three thousand in recent years.

A few weeks after his announcement, Gary had a previously scheduled breakfast with Terry Crist of the smaller but growing CitiChurch, which had twelve hundred in attendance in nearby Scottsdale. At breakfast Gary shared with Terry that he was looking for a younger but seasoned and successful pastor who would follow him at Word of Grace: "Someone a lot like you." Gary then asked Terry, "Can you recommend anyone?"

Terry's response took Gary by surprise. "I have someone to recommend: me." Gary responded incredulously, "You would leave your church in Scottsdale to pastor mine?" "No, I would become the pastor of both congregations," Terry responded.

That initial conversation developed into a prayerful, nine-month, intense interaction between the senior leadership teams of the two congregations. It culminated in a unanimous decision of both teams to become one church in two locations under one vision, a new name, and a new senior pastor. City of Grace is today a flourishing multisite church because of a successful succession-driven merger.

A parallel smaller church example is a story we develop in Chapter Six. The pastor of a small-attendance church initiated a merger discussion because, in part, he was ready to move on, ideally to plant a new church. He thought the merger would give his congregation a better future and also create a larger financial base for sending him out and supporting him to plant a church in a new city.

The biggest elephant in church boardrooms in the United States is the topic of senior pastor succession. It is a difficult conversation for most aging senior pastors to have with their boards and staff, so usually it is ignored until too late. Many are predicting a tsunami of church turnovers

> *The biggest elephant in church boardrooms in the United States is the topic of senior pastor succession.*

during the next decade as the aging baby boomers turn over the reins of US churches to the next generation. According to William Vanderbloemen, founder and president of the Vanderbloemen Search Group, senior pastor succession "might be the biggest unspoken crisis the church in the US will face over the next twenty years."[8]

Often when a pastor retires or leaves a church due to health reasons, the church is thrown into a tailspin to find a successor. The search is usually led by lay leaders who do not know how to find or interview senior pastor candidates. Meanwhile, the church stalls or declines in the interim period while the pastor search is in process. Often a new pastor comes and begins all over again with a new vision, abandoning all the vestiges of the previous pastor's philosophy. There's got to be a better way! As these two pastor succession stories illustrate, a church merger could be a vehicle for a seamless senior pastor succession that keeps the church moving forward without losing momentum and upsetting the equilibrium of a healthy church.

Reconciliation-Driven Hope

Mariners Church, Irvine, California, held its first service as a church in a home in 1965. The church continued to grow over the years, and then in 1980 the church split because of a leadership conflict. The pastor at the time created a new church with a new name only a few miles away. Even though the two churches were separated by only a few miles, they ministered independently. This situation generated a lot of pain and sadness.

Then in 1995, under the leadership of Kenton Beshore, God began to guide the paths of these two churches toward each other once again in an amazing reunion and mutual commitment to serve Orange County as one church body. In 1998, the two churches came back together as one. To this day, Mariners Church has continued to spread the gospel, transforming ordinary people into passionate followers of Jesus, courageously changing the world.

In another example, Christ Community Church was launched in Ruston, Louisiana, in 1984 as a plant of Fellowship Bible Church in Little Rock, Arkansas. In 1995, Christ Community Church experienced a deep and painful split following a prolonged leadership conflict. The founding elders left the church along with a number of other families, and the senior staff remained along with a new elder board and continued shepherding the large number of families that stayed.

Six years later, in 2001, two of the original elders who left Christ Community began meeting with a small group of people to begin exploring launching a new Fellowship Bible church plant in Ruston. In 2003, Crossroads Church was officially launched just a few miles away from Christ Community. For five years, these two church plants of Fellowship Bible Church coexisted in the same small college town.

By 2008, Crossroads had grown to three hundred adults plus two hundred college students in worship. They met in multiple services in a gym that holds only 375 chairs. Christ Community had an attendance of 350 in a new worship space that was built in 2005 to hold six hundred seats.

That same year, Wade Burnett, the executive pastor of Crossroads Church, initiated a dialogue with the pastor of Christ Community Church. Wade explained in a local newspaper interview, "We met for coffee and ended up having a three-hour conversation. We apologized to one another for having been so prideful and foolish for all those years. That meeting led to similar conversations with the other leaders," which culminated in a public reconciliation service in 2010. The elders from both churches—including those who were involved in the split in 1995—publicly shared the full forgiveness and grace they had extended to one another over the preceding two years. The service concluded with the leadership from Fellowship Bible Church serving communion to all of the reconciled elders and the elders in turn serving communion to the body who was gathered together. Because the whole community had been affected by what Wade called this "bitter conflict," they posted this powerful story of reconciliation and healing online at www .thereconciliation.info.[9]

A year later the two churches voted overwhelmingly to reunite under a new name and a reorganized leadership team incorporating staff and elders from both congregations. Wade Burnett, who initiated the reconciliation as the executive pastor of Crossroads Church, became the directional leader and the two senior pastors became teaching pastors of The Bridge Community Church. Building on the momentum of coming together, the merged church is now meeting in two locations while pursuing a new and much larger vision of serving as a multisite, church-planting church for its entire region.

What began as a reconciliation effort ended in a church reunion merger and a stronger corporate ministry with the potential to reach an entire region with the gospel. The rebirth and recasting of a much larger vision never would have happened without the fruits of a deep and very personal reconciliation.

The Takeaway   Church splits are always painful, especially when they involve disagreements that could have been resolved or conflicts that were ungodly or inappropriate. These less-than-noble church splits give the church a black eye in their communities and foster cynicism about our failures to walk our talk and genuinely live out our faith. But what better public statement could there be than for churches who have split from one another—and specifically the leaders of churches who may have been involved in these kinds of conflicts—to come back together in biblical restoration and reconciliation? Many times, this kind of spiritual transformation provides a foundation for much greater kingdom impact.

Unfortunately too many churches were born unintentionally as the result of a church split. It is the authors' hope that this book will encourage potentially thousands of churches across the United States that were birthed out of conflict to seek reconciliation, whether or not those dialogues result in a reunified congregation.

Many of these conversations could develop into a reconciliation-based merger. In such mergers, typically a leader from one of the congregations initiates a reconciliation conversation. One phone call can put in motion a healing of relationships that could result in a reunification of two estranged congregations. One meeting over a cup of coffee could transform the church landscape in your community. Sometimes reconciliation mergers become one church in two locations (multisite) and other times they come back together in one location. Regardless, the driving motivation is healing and can result in reconciliation. Is a reconciliation merger in your future?

Desire to Be Multiethnic

US churches are becoming increasingly multicultural. Though the most segregated hour in the United States historically has been the 11:00 church service on Sunday mornings, the times are a-changing. According to a recent *Time* magazine article, "the proportion of American churches with 20% or more minority participation has languished at about 7.5% for the past nine years. But among evangelical churches with attendance of 1,000 people or more, the slice has more than quadrupled, from 6% in 1998 to 25% in 2007."[10]

A growing number of emerging church leaders desire to see their congregations reflect on earth what we will all experience in heaven—a sea of diverse races, languages, and colors all worshipping Jesus *together*. Those leaders work hard at being inclusive by preaching racial equality, building multiracial staffs, integrating worship teams, and serving their communities across racial and ethnic divides.

Some immigrant churches are merging together so that all generations can be under one roof. For example, in 2007 the English-only ministry of a predominantly Hispanic church merged with a Spanish-only ministry formerly known as *Centro de Restoration* (Restoration Center) making it possible to accommodate the needs

> *One of the most dramatic and accelerated ways to become a truly multiethnic church is by incorporating a minority congregation through a church merger.*

of multiple generations of Latinos in one church.[11] Others are finding that one of the most dramatic and accelerated ways to become a truly multiethnic church is by incorporating a minority congregation through a church merger.

One example of this mission-driven merger is beautifully illustrated by the multiethnic Mosaic Church in Little Rock, Arkansas. In 2008 senior pastor Mark DeYmaz invited a struggling Hispanic church with two full-time pastors to join his leadership team, share his facility, and provide a third service of Mosaic Church. The pastors agreed to work on their weekly sermon together with the intent that each would communicate roughly the same message as the other. The third service then featured the message in Spanish by the Hispanic pastors, and Pastor Mark delivered the same sermon in English at the other two services. This arrangement provided a service for immigrants who speak Spanish only, and it also offered additional options to those Latino attendees and their spouses who would prefer English services over Spanish. Mark solved a problem of many ethnic churches that start in the native language of a first-generation immigrant, but typically the second and third generations of an immigrant family prefer an English service as they move into the mainstream of US culture. Both options are now available to all Latino attendees, all under one roof and one church.

As in any successful merger, it was important to clarify for both congregations what this new relationship would look like. Leading up to the official merger with Mosaic, the pastors of the two congregations distributed a document defining the new relationship. Here is what they published on the day of the merger.

Merger of Iglesia Nazareno del Samaritano and the Mosaic Church of Central Arkansas

What It Is

1. It is an official merger between Iglesia Nazareno del Samaritano and the Mosaic Church of Central Arkansas whereby from now on we will all be known as the Mosaic Church of Central Arkansas.
2. It is an opportunity for expanded, more effective evangelism of first-generation Latinos via Mosaic.
3. It is an opportunity for more effective evangelism of second- and third-generation Latinos via Mosaic.

What It Is Not

1. We are not two churches under one roof. We are one church, now with multiple service options.
2. It does not in any way change our DNA. Rather, it eliminates a barrier we unintentionally established through the years, namely, one that made it difficult for many first-generation Latinos to find Christ and/or a church home with us at Mosaic.
3. It is not an exclusive or intentional segregation of people by ethnic heritage or language, etc. Anyone and everyone is welcome to attend any of Mosaic's worship services or program options![12]

This merger was driven by both pastors' passion and mission to build a truly multiethnic church. Mark described the benefits to us in this way:

Such a merger, when rightly conceived and executed, will be beneficial to both churches. On the one hand, homogeneous churches that are pursing the multi-ethnic vision will immediately benefit from the addition of diverse staff and people to the mix, and the merger provides a visible sign of their commitment to transformation. On the other hand, the 1.0 (first generation) congregation will often benefit from the additional ministries provided, including children's or student ministry more in line with the integrated schools their kids are likely attending.

Mark insists that his motive was not to seek out a merger but to support whatever God was doing. "Our attitude and mind-set was to have an open hand with helping churches," he told us, "and when it led to the idea of merging, we were open to it." But to no one's surprise, when an opportunity came up in 2011 for another merger, and the mission fit was good, Mark and the church's leadership enthusiastically explored and followed it as well.

Rarely a Single Motive

In most cases, a merger represents a blending of many of these motives at different levels. A case in point is a wonderful ceremony that took place in downtown Baton Rouge, Louisiana. On that day in April 2010, Winbourne Avenue Baptist Church's one-thousand-seat sanctuary was the fullest it had been in decades. The church, established in 1947, had declined in recent years to fewer than twenty-five elderly people on a typical Sunday but on this day over four hundred came, many from different parts of the country. They celebrated all God had done over the years as they now offered their church facilities as a gift to become the Dream Center campus for Healing Place Church. This was their final service with their own pastor, and the legal paperwork for the merger would be finalized two months later.

Meanwhile, since 2008 the Dream Center had been holding its own worship service there, drawing up to two hundred people from the community and launching numerous ministries including free groceries for those who need it, child care for all ages, a free clothing center, re-entry programs for ex-offenders, a street outreach for homeless and at-risk youth, and after-school programs including computer and GED courses for teenagers. On Sunday mornings a van would patrol the neighborhood, picking up families for a free meal served from the church's large kitchen before the Healing Place's noon service began.

In this merger of Winbourne Avenue Baptist and the Healing Place Dream Center, the missional motive showed up strongly in both churches whose congregations were enthusiastic about continuing the mandates of scripture into the future. "You could say we are passing the torch," Eugene Coffing, chair of the Winbourne Baptist deacon board, told a local newspaper. "Healing Place is reaching out to the people in the surrounding neighborhoods for Christ, and they are doing it effectively."

"From my perspective, Winbourne Avenue Baptist was given a vision and a dream to start a church here in 1947, and they have been shining the light of the Gospel here ever since," added Craig Boutte, Healing Place pastor at the Winbourne Dream Center. "They are passing the torch to us because we also know God has a purpose for this area." Melvin Hardnett, a local businessman who coordinates the Dream Center's more than one hundred volunteers, agreed with his pastor. "They (the Baptist group) started the race and now we are going to cross the finish line," Hardnett said.

Dino Rizzo, lead pastor at Healing Place Church, agrees, saying, "The great hearts of a group of people at Winbourne Baptist Church followed what they felt was God's leading to give us their facility to use for spreading the Gospel through the Baton Rouge Dream Center."

The economic pressure was primarily with the Winbourne Avenue congregation as their dwindling numbers could no longer fund the property costs. But Healing Place also faced economic challenges, wanting to do ministry but not being able to build or purchase something like the Winbourne Avenue facility, valued at $2 million. They too were looking for a win.

The multisite factor was only on Healing Place's side. It was founded in 1993 and just nine years later opened its first offsite campus. By the time the Winbourne Baptist opportunity opened up, Healing Place already had eleven different campuses, two of them overseas. The US campuses were already drawing over seven thousand people each weekend. Although this was its first Dream Center campus, the church clearly understood how to do effective ministry as one church in multiple locations.

The reconciliation factor was minimal. The two churches, one Baptist and the other nondenominational charismatic, had not previously been partnered together. Nor had there been any division in which a contingent from one church was now attending the other. However, reconciliation did occur at two other levels. First in 2007, the pastor at the time, after learning as much as possible about Healing Place Church, initiated contact, inviting its leadership to come on the Winbourne Avenue property and begin using some of the facility for ministry in that area. His hope was that the Winbourne Baptist congregation would eventually turn the property over to Healing Place. Second, through the Dream Center, bridges were built from the church, which was largely white as the community once was, to the community that is now racially mixed.

Of all six merger motivations, perhaps the strongest affirmation of all was a six-word message displayed on the day of the special service. Up on the sanctuary platform, just below the baptistery, a wide-screen TV declared the Healing Place theme in bold yellow letters: "Jesus is here, anything can happen."

Part Two

HOW HEALTHY CHURCH MERGERS WORK

4

STAGES AND SPEED
OF A MERGER

The ten-week time between our announcement
and the vote seems to have helped put most people
at ease because they feel there is ample time to
make an informed and prayer-based decision. As
you would expect, comments have ranged from,
"It's about time!" to "How could you?"

—Comment from a church leader
interviewed for this book

Every church is different in the speed it follows when exploring a merger. We find it helpful to view the merger as happening in five different stages and then to estimate the speed of each stage based on your circumstances:

- *Exploration* is like dating as you assess the possibility of merging.
- *Negotiation* is like courtship as you determine the feasibility of a merger.
- *Implementation* is like engagement as you make a public announcement.
- *Consolidation* is like a wedding as the union takes place, typically including a new name for the church.
- *Integration* is like a marriage as the two congregations begin the hard work of learning how to live together as one church.

For Woodside Bible Church in greater Detroit, which has done five mergers to date—all of a rebirth or adoption model—the exploration stage always started with a conversation over coffee. "Our senior pastor, Doug Schmidt, has a burden to encourage and consult with other local churches to help them be as effective as possible. As a result, his phone rings about once a week with an area pastor calling and asking for help in some way," says Beth McKenna, the church's campus development director. "His heart is to help other pastors however he can. A lot of pastors have called on him over his twenty years with us, and a few of those have led to mergers. Merging is not so much a strategy for us but a way we're continually helping other congregations."

> "Merging is not so much a strategy for us but a way we're continually helping other congregations," says Beth McKenna

Woodside's first merger was in 2006. A pastor located about thirty minutes away said, "We're going to have to sell our building. We're not going to make it." Doug asked why. They talked and prayed. "What if we come in and help rebuild the ministry?" Doug asked.

"We clearly communicated that we will infuse our DNA and it will become a Woodside Bible Church in a new location," Beth explains. Today almost five hundred people meet at that campus of Woodside Bible.

During the negotiation process, each party affirms what things are musts for them, and they evaluate their compatibility to determine whether they should take the next step toward a merger. Woodside's approach is to replace the senior pastor of each church that merges with them. "They are welcome to reapply for different positions at Woodside but there are no guarantees. While we do our best to honor and help transition staff, they know that our priority is to make the decisions that will best rebuild this ministry," says Beth. "At the end of the day the joining church is saying 'yes' to new leadership. We're not looking for an arrangement that's a little of them and a little of us."

The joining church brings its non-negotiables as well. For example, Woodside's second merger, about forty minutes away, was arguably the most influential church in Michigan back in the 1940s. It was one of the country's early megachurches. It started fifteen branch Sunday schools over the years. The church building had aged and was to be torn down, so some of the leaders removed a stained glass window, intending to install it in their new building. As a way of honoring a ministry that's existed for some 185 years, they asked Woodside to place it in the addition that was planned for this campus. "We said absolutely yes," Beth says.

Woodside has developed a series of internal criteria that also help it discern if it should proceed with the merger opportunity. The questions include the following:

- *Are we healthy enough financially to take on this ministry?* This requires disclosure by the lead church and joining church about debts, any active litigation, and so on.

- *Is it more than twenty minutes from our other campuses?* Woodside leadership wants people to commit to one campus. They don't want to create an unintentional competition that invites people to float, depending on what's going on at each campus.

- *Is the senior pastor, if still present, willing to relocate?* Woodside doesn't leave the senior pastor there. "We believe the people need a new leader, one who knows and has experienced Woodside's DNA," Beth explains. "Merging is difficult enough so our preference is to move one of our Woodside pastors into leadership. Very early on in the process we'll confirm with the joining church pastor, 'You understand that if we go through with this, it will require you to transition to another ministry.' If the pastor's desire is still to proceed, we will assist him in finding another ministry, invite him to apply for a ministry position at another Woodside campus, or severance him," Beth explains.

- *Are the church cultures compatible?* This involves asking how difficult is it for the existing body to blend with us, whether both churches' doctrines are the same and sense of mission similar, and is the organizational structure workable. "Take a close look at their ministry and see if there are enough similarities to make the 'marriage' work," Beth says.

- *As Woodside takes the lead, will the leaders of the struggling ministry agree that the former way of doing ministry will come to an end?* The existing board and congregation need to be in agreement with the fact that Woodside will come in and begin to rebuild the ministry and infuse its DNA. This is critical to a new beginning and the success of the campus, Woodside feels. "We treat them with honor and respect but we also need to be permitted to lead them forward," Beth says.

- *Is there enough growth potential at this time?* There are always enough unchurched people to reach in any community, but does the combination of the lead church and joining church offer a strong enough base of people and leaders needed for a strong relaunch of the joining church?

Woodside offers numerous opportunities to talk about the merger and to meet with the elders for questions and answers (Q&A). A series of FAQs are developed and circulated (reprinted in Appendix E).

Typically both Woodside and the joining church take a congregational vote. "We want the votes to go through without surprises, and we communicate with the congregation well enough so that the people are prepared," Beth says.

During the implementation stage, Woodside works especially hard to overcommunicate the benefits. In Woodside's approach, each merger represents a new campus, and so mergers are positioned as part of its multisite strategy. "Each time we have posted a merger opportunity or written about it in our newspaper we tend to include this list of advantages for people to read," says Beth, drawing from material they've gleaned from other multisite churches.

Multicampus Ministry Advantages at Woodside Bible Church

Increased outreach: When churches expand to multiple locations, they dramatically increase their outreach. When Leadership Network surveyed one thousand multisite churches, the number-one reason churches added new sites was for evangelistic purposes. This strategy enables us to fulfill our vision. Campuses can and will birth other campuses in neighboring communities.

Increased resources: Campuses can come together to share ideas and encourage one another. Multiple campuses provide a broad base of leaders to strategize with and learn from. They can share ministry resources while still developing local leadership and ownership.

Involved followers: When you reproduce [add more campuses], you involve more people in ministry and many people actually reengage because church is now closer to their neighborhood. Researchers have found that if a campus is more than twenty minutes away from their home, people will drive to join the weekly worship service but their ability to serve and to invite friends is diminished.

Improved quality: Each time we launch a new site, we rethink how we do ministry and this improves quality. Because certain overhead and personnel expenses are shared, costs tend to drop. Also, centers of excellence emerge. For example, one campus may develop an effective neighborhood group strategy that we decide to share and implement at other campuses.

Improved leaders: Multicampus ministry increases leadership development. The most successful multisite leaders have been home grown. Developing staff from within the congregation works well and certainly fits the biblical model.

The consolidation of the merger happens quickly for Woodside. Some merger efforts close the joining church campus for a time. Woodside does not. "We step in and immediately care for the congregation," Beth says. "The day after the ink is dry we arrive with donuts and coffee. We want to get to know them and their stories. Our primary focus is the Sunday worship service because we need to be ready in a week. Although we are 'open,' we take two to three months to infuse our DNA and then we go public in terms of announcing the merger to the community."

Finally, the integration takes time with bumps expected. "We advise, 'Don't expect everyone to be supportive until about eighteen months.' It's an emotional time. People are both glad and are hurting."

But over time the integration happens. In Woodside's five mergers, a majority of the people have stayed. At first it's "You guys" or "Woodside says." Then it's "Our ministry is alive again." At the end of the day, people begin talking like they're at the same church and in the same blended family—which they are.

Three Big Questions

There are three big questions to address in a merger process that frame the merger conversation:

- Is this merger *possible*? Determine if a merger is a possibility through a conversation between the senior pastors and the church boards. This results in a recommendation to begin merger deliberations.
- Is this merger *feasible*? Determine the compatibility of the two congregations through due diligence in addressing all the issues. This results in a recommendation to both congregations to merge or not to merge.
- Is this merger *desirable*? This becomes apparent as the churches go through a process of meetings to discuss the idea of merging, which culminates in a churchwide vote or poll.

Though no analogy is perfect, the marriage analogy is help-ful, but it implies equality of two partners, which is rarely the case in church mergers. As we mentioned previously, most church mergers involve a lead church and a joining church. The lead church is the stronger and usually the larger church.

When the senior leaders of two congregations conclude that the potential benefits of merging outweigh the drawbacks of going their separate ways, then the merger deliberations process can begin. Most happen quickly and are done within a year; some can take longer. There are a lot of moving parts, but a church merger can be broken down into five basic stages. Although this process is more art than science, each stage addresses a specific question. The time frames can vary but gen-erally they fall into the following stages.

Exploration and Dating (One to Two Months)

Merger deliberations usually begin between the two senior pas-tors or acting leaders. One of the most important questions to answer at this stage is whether the pastor of the joining church pastor will be retained or replaced. This is a delicate issue that can cause the joining church to feel rejected or to resent the lead church if its pastor is not retained. After working through this and other exploratory issues, if both churches become con-vinced that a merger possibility is worthwhile to consider, then the two senior leadership teams are brought into the discussion to determine, "Is this possible?"

Negotiation and Courtship (One to Two Months)

The best merger possibilities occur when there is at least an 80 percent DNA match between the two congregations in doc-trine, philosophy of ministry, and ministry style. Like any good marriage, the more in common, the better the chances of suc-cess. But sometimes, as in a good marriage, the right combina-tion of opposites have a strong attraction to each other such as a suburban church seeking more meaningful engagement with an economically challenged area and a downtown church surrounded by need but lacking in resources to make it happen.

The two leadership teams should keep the discussion confidential if possible until they agree that merging is feasible. In most churches, any public hint of a merger before the leadership can determine feasibility will often undermine the process before it even has a chance to be seriously considered.

The two senior leadership teams need to identify the issues, create a due diligence checklist to discern the DNA match, and design a timeline to determine the feasibility. (Twenty-five issues that need to be addressed are explained in Chapter Twelve.) This stage culminates in a recommendation by both leadership teams to merge or not to merge.

Implementation and Engagement (One to Three Months)

This phase begins with a recommendation to merge to both congregations by both leadership teams, accompanied with a FAQs document. This is followed by congregational town halls at both congregations, culminating in a congregational vote or poll by the joining church, if not both congregations. The outcome of the votes will reveal, "Is this desirable?"

During this time the lead church needs to drive the communication strategy and evaluate each ministry area of the joining church to determine what and when to integrate, recalibrate, or eliminate if the merger is approved. The key to successful mergers is establishing the postmerger leadership team and integration process before the merger is approved.

The key to successful mergers is establishing the postmerger leadership team and integration process before the merger is approved.

Consolidation and Wedding (Two to Four Weeks)

Phased integration of two congregations becoming one church usually occurs within two to four weeks after the vote is approved. The two congregations become one church in an inaugural joint service. The joining church is usually dissolved and celebrates its final service the week prior to the inaugural service. Sometimes there may be a longer hiatus of a few weeks or even months between the final service and the inaugural service due to necessary renovation or retooling. Occasionally there needs to be an emotional and physical separation in order to get full closure before beginning a new chapter. The new chapter for both congregations does not begin with a question, but a statement, "We're doing it!"

Integration and Marriage (Three to Six Months Later)

It usually takes one to three years for two congregations to move through the "yours, mine, and ours" phases of a merger marriage. The first few months are the most crucial to long-term success and can be the most traumatic. The new church entity needs to establish quickly who's in charge, a clear reporting structure, and integrated systems. It is helpful initially to have monthly postmerger evaluations of staff, ministries, congregation, attendance, and finances to answer the question, "How are we doing?"

Adoption mergers tend to move quickly. Reconciliation-based mergers tend to move more slowly because relational healing takes time. Full integration typically takes longer in larger and older joining congregations.

Here is a checklist of things to do postmerger:

In the Days Immediately After a Decision to Merge

- Announce the decision through e-mail, twitter, the website, and a bulletin. Overcommunicate.

- Have senior leaders review and discuss Chapter Four, "Stages and Speed of a Merger" and Chapter Five, "How to Measure Success" from this book.

- Host a celebratory elder or church board gathering within the first week and review the strategy for the next three months.

- Host a celebratory all-staff meeting within the first week to reaffirm the direction and review the next three months.

- Review and begin acting on all steps indicated in the Merger FAQ document you created, updating it and other documents online, and informing local media.

- Begin executing new systems and procedures immediately, always overcommunicating to preclude misunderstandings.

- Complete planning for the final worship celebration at the joining church and the inaugural worship services of the combined congregation.

- Install new signage the week following the final celebration service at the joining church, again overcommunicating to preclude any unnecessary hurt feelings. (Planning for new signage should begin before the merger vote and ordered as soon as the merger decision is official so as to be ready to install at this point.)

- If you intend to keep the joining church facility as a campus, install the new campus pastor on the inaugural Sunday.

- Update website, brochures, and e-mail addresses to reflect the new entity within first month of the completed merger.

- Complete the legal due diligence.

- Complete the reorganization of staff, ministries, and offices within three months of the approved merger.

- Complete any facility improvements within three to six months of the approved merger.

Not Always Sequential

Not all merger proposals go forward on their first exploration. Sometimes they never go through. Sometimes the initial conversation doesn't go very far but then gets picked up months or even years later.

When the idea of merging with another church was first discussed among the forty or so members of Interbay Covenant Church in downtown Seattle, discussions grew heated. Their longtime pastor, age sixty-one, had announced plans to move on, but few welcomed the idea of the change that inevitably accompanies a merger. Some had been members of the church for a good portion of its sixty-five-year life. Many were predictably wary of giving away their property, losing their style, and closing the book on so many years of vibrant history. The idea was shelved but it resurfaced months later, again prompted by their pastor's plan to complete his ministry there.

The idea was to join a church named Quest that had been renting space from Interbay for some time. Both were multiethnic and both were part of the same denomination. But Quest was young: founded in 2001, its pastor was young (age thirty-six at the time), the congregation was young (mostly in their twenties and thirties and heavily single), and its music was loud.

Barbara Lundquist, seventy-three, who has served as chairwoman of the Interbay congregation, said people questioned Quest. "They said, 'Who are they? How long have they been a church? Come on, we're giving them our church?'" she reported.

Two years separated the initial discussion and completed merger, but after much discussion and prayer, Interbay members voted to give their multimillion-dollar property to Quest and fold into their larger neighbor.

"We saw within Quest a freshness, a vibrancy, a vision for the city of Seattle and beyond that was very appealing to us. It spoke to us," said Interbay's outgoing pastor, Ray Bartel. "We wanted to add our facilities and resources to theirs, to add to what they're already doing well in connecting to the next generation."

"It really is an amazing, incredulous story," said Eugene Cho, pastor of Quest. "It's very humbling to me. It's very sacrificial."

Ray and Eugene agree that the merger was driven by a commitment to the larger kingdom of God. What Interbay was doing was "giving ourselves to the next generation," Ray Bartel added.

The brick church building with soaring curved beams, amber windows, beige walls, and a red curtain covering its baptistery may change a bit in its appearance. But the church itself will continue to make a difference in its community for yet another generation.[1]

Overcommunicate at Every Stage

Perhaps the strongest message in the comments people made in the Leadership Network 2011 survey of church mergers is the need for the joining and lead churches to communicate better at every stage in the process. As one person explained with great passion, "Communicate, communicate, communicate! With pastors, elders, leaders, and the congregation itself, talk to them all and then talk some more."

One of the most helpful tools for communication is a FAQs document, as mentioned previously in this chapter, and made available to a church's entire constituency, both online and in print. We provide several examples of effective FAQs in the appendixes. These are the typical issues to address in such as document:

Sample FAQs

- How did this merger idea come about?
- Why are we considering a merger?
- What are the benefits of this proposed merger?

- What is the timeline for this proposed merger?
- Who will be our pastor?
- What will happen to each church's pastor and staff?
- How will the new (merged) church be staffed?
- What will the worship services be like?
- How will the budget and finances be managed?
- Will our church have a new name and what will it be?
- How will current membership be transferred?
- Who will decide if this merger happens?
- If the merger happens, what will change?
- What will the merger cost? Can we afford it?
- What will happen to each church's facilities?
- What will happen if the merger doesn't go through?
- What are *my* next steps?

Though we have suggested sequential stages and time frames for the merger process, we acknowledge again that church mergers are messy. No two church mergers are alike. Each one has a unique set of circumstances and fingerprint—or "church-print"—but all will go through similar stages. Some will go back and forth through these stages, some will go faster, and others will take longer. The important thing is to work through these stages carefully and as thoroughly as possible and with integrity.

5

HOW TO MEASURE SUCCESS

What does a successful merger look like? Like many pastors, Will Marotti enjoys getting to know fellow clergy in his community. Will had initiated a monthly prayer gathering of area ministers, and it met on occasion in the former pharmacy that housed his growing congregation, New Life Church, Meriden, Connecticut. As the pastors prayed for their community and the general needs of their respective churches, Will would ask the others to pray with him for a better location because theirs was overcrowded week after week.

At the conclusion of the December 2005 prayer meeting, a pastor pulled Will aside. "What if our two churches merged?" he asked Will. Seeing Will's puzzled face, he made his case. "You've got no space here and you are busting at the seams; we have lots of space and we're not growing." The pastor also confided that he'd like to move on to plant a new church, and maybe the merger would make that possible. So they talked further, prayed, and agreed to raise the matter with their respective church boards.

Both boards found the idea appealing. The church with the ample facility was part of a denomination, and its denominational leaders were delighted that Will's nondenominational congregation was willing to affiliate with them, instantly making it their largest church in the area.

Just months beforehand, New Life had already experienced an informal adoption merger. It had gone very well. The lay leader of a large Hispanic cell group had asked to be enfolded into New Life. The process went simply and quickly. There were no assets to transfer. They were the joining congregation and New Life was the lead congregation. The union gave New

Life a Spanish language outreach in a city with one of the fastest growing Hispanic populations in Connecticut. New Life brought the pastor of the Hispanic church on its staff part time. The Hispanic church's volunteer worship leader became New Life's worship leader, a role he would stay in for the next several years.

Will trusted that the second merger would go as smoothly, with his church again serving in the lead church role, and so within a few months plans were finalized for the new, more formal merger. Most of the discussion and excitement surrounded the vision of being able to reach the community for Christ far better together than separately.

The congregations began to get to know each other. The joining church agreed to take on New Life's name and leadership. New Life would move into its 250-seat facility on seven acres. New Life would keep the pharmacy building and open a daycare center there.

All seemed to go well until the third Sunday after the merger. Will wanted to be physically closer to the people as he preached. In the drugstore that had been converted into a house of worship, he had used a small podium and positioned it somewhat close to the first row of the congregation. The church's new location had a high platform with huge furniture that felt like an obstacle to Will.

So just before the morning worship service he snagged a couple of burly men and asked them to move the communion table into a nearby storage room. The table wasn't needed that day because neither church served communion every week. By moving the table, Will would now have room to preach on the floor immediately in front of the first pews—which now had lots of people in them for the first time in years.

That quick decision soon became the rally point of opposition for certain members of the congregation who had worshipped there for so many years. "Look what those people are doing to our church," one influential elder said as he began to look for others who didn't like the changes that New Life had brought with it.

In the coming months about half of the smaller church left to go to other churches. The former pastor, who remained supportive of the merger and had worked hard to quell the unrest, was commissioned and financially supported by New Life for several years as he moved to another town and planted a new church. New Life weathered the pain of the criticisms, continued to grow, and today has a thriving outreach to the community— even becoming multisite by renting an auditorium for weekly services in the town next door.

Pastor Will regrets the pain he caused by his hasty decision to move the communion table. "I didn't realize the hurt it would cause," he says. "If I could do it again, I'd still replace a lot of the furniture, but I'd prepare the people and walk them through the change."

But Will has no regrets for saying yes to the merger. He continues to believe—as does the joining church's pastor—that the pathway to combine the two congregations is a door that God opened. "We wouldn't be where we are today without help from mergers," Will says. "Our mergers broadened the ministry impact of our church in significant ways."

> *Our mergers broadened the ministry impact of our church in significant ways.*

Will also wishes he had known a bit more in advance about mergers. His training and early career were in the automotive industry. He and his wife, both longtime followers of Christ, had been active in a church and had learned much about ministry there. When Will sensed God's call into full-time ministry, his pastor invited him to come on staff as associate pastor. Will also served as a volunteer hospital chaplain, northeast director of Evangelism Explosion, and state coordinator for the National Day of Prayer in Connecticut. These were all good experiences, but church mergers were a new idea—how would he know what success looks like beyond the overall vision of reaching more people and making more disciples of Christ?

"My filter is to ask if it expands God's kingdom by bringing more people to Christ," Will says. Beyond that ideal, how could he gauge the effectiveness of the churches that had united together?

Measuring Merger Success

Based on the Leadership Network 2011 survey of merger churches like New Life, we'd like to propose the following measurable standards as a way to define and measure a church merger's success. Will Marotti's experience in this chapter represents an adoption merger, but the benchmarks we propose can apply to the four types of mergers introduced in Chapters Two and Three: rebirths, adoptions, marriages, and ICU mergers.

Stabilize

Within one year of the merger, the church's leadership will have created a new congregational culture that embraces the merger, focuses on the future, provides financial steadiness, and sustains an attendance equal to or greater than that of the combined attendance of the two church bodies prior to the merger. The board and congregation's corporate self-esteem will point to the future, viewing the life of the new congregation as "the best years are yet to come."

Grow in People and Finances

Within three years of the merger, the attendance and the financial base will each have grown by at least 10 percent. Further, new attendees will more closely represent the median age, race, and economic levels of the surrounding community as compared to the church demographics in either congregation prior to the merger.

Be Able to Replicate

Within five years of the merger, more than half the committees, ministries, and programs will be composed of people who
joined after the merger and have embodied the church's heart
of outreach to the point that they are moving toward reproducing another congregation, whether by another merger, a church
plant, a satellite site, or another missional entity.

As our friend and seasoned church consultant David
Schmidt reminded us when he read an early draft of this book,
two hundred stuck Christians in one church that merge with
one hundred stuck Christians in another church gives you
three hundred stuck Christians—just in one place together.
Economies of scale that
come from a merger do
not necessarily translate
into a better church.
As he told us when he
reviewed our manu-
script, "If the new min-
istry strategy merely blends two old ones that weren't effective
in the first place, then you really haven't gained new ground in
moving people toward Jesus."

Economies of scale that come from a merger do not necessarily translate into a better church.

The real measure of success of a merger is seen after the
merger is in the rearview mirror of both churches. The ultimate
goal is for the congregation to grow in its outreach, service, and
Christlikeness. As Acts 2:42 reminds us, a biblically functioning
community should be one marked by believers who are devoting
themselves "to the apostles' teaching and to the fellowship, to
the breaking of bread and to prayer." Acts 2 gives us a beautiful snapshot and goal to aspire to of a healthy congregation in
which the people are "praising God and enjoying the favor of all
the people" and where the Lord is adding to their number daily
"those who were being saved" (Acts 2:47). Table 5.1 summarizes
these three sets of mile markers.

Table 5.1   Setting Milestones Helps You Define Success as a Merger

One Year	Three Years	Five Years
Mission and vision: Emphasis is more on the future than the past.	All "signature" ministries are fully integrated under a unified vision and leadership and nonstrategic ministries are eliminated.	Plans are in motion to continue reproducing, whether by another merger, a church plant, a satellite site, or another missional entity.
Integration: Majority feels merger was good thing to do.	Attendees no longer see themselves as "us" and "them" but as "we." At least half of the church's committees, ministries, and programs are made up of people who joined after the merger.	Retention of at least half of the original attendance of the merged congregation
Attendance: Attendance is at least equal to combination of both churches before the merger.	Attendance has grown by at least 10 percent more than the combination of both churches before the merger. Newcomers since the merger match surrounding community more closely than church demographics prior to the merger.	Facility maximized with multiple worship services and 80 percent capacity at the optimal inviting hour
Finances: Giving is at least equal to a combination of both churches before the merger.	Giving has grown by at least 10 percent more than the combination of both churches before the merger.	Additional funds are raised for church expansion.
Community impact: Perception of the church by the community moves from negative to positive.	The church proactively engages the community with externally focused ministries.	The church becomes a recognized strategic partner in community transformation

Comparison with the Business World

Businesses merge in order to experience a net gain in effectiveness, market share, influence, and financial gain—especially the last. Should any of those values be true for churches?

One marketplace book on corporate mergers[1] tells the story of two banks in discussion about a merger. One of the bank presidents, who was the point person for the negotiations, was concerned that his employees would be treated fairly should the merger take place, but those overseeing the merger didn't care about the people element. The human side of the merger, he was told, should not be a consideration beyond one person: "The only position you should consider is that of the owner," a member of the board of directors instructed him.

By contrast, Will Marotti was all about people development in the two mergers he oversaw. "The whole point of a merger is to develop people as disciples of Christ and to make it possible for more people to experience the love of Christ," he says. Although corporate takeovers, mergers, and acquisitions are fundamentally motivated by a financial bottom line, the ultimate goal of a church merger is lives transformed by Jesus Christ.

Although corporate takeovers, mergers, and acquisitions are fundamentally motivated by a financial bottom line, the ultimate goal of a church merger is lives transformed by Jesus Christ.

Even with such a contrast, it may be helpful to compare church mergers and business mergers. As Table 5.2 demonstrates, church and marketplace mergers must deal with the same issues, though the goals and outcomes may differ.

Table 5.2   Church Mergers Are Different from Business Mergers

Factor	Marketplace	Church
Prompted by a crisis	Sometimes	Often
Initiated by the smaller organization	Rarely	Usually
Motivated by desire for financial gain	Always	Rarely
Success measured primarily in economic terms	Always	Rarely
Proposed as a win for both organizations	Sometimes	Usually
Involves a vote by the shareholders (business) or membership (church)	Rarely	Usually
Involves a vote by the employees or staff	Rarely	Usually
Involves a vote by the governing board	Always	Always
Involves outside consultant(s)	Usually	Sometimes
Involves asset transfers	Always	Always
Involves personnel changes	Always	Usually
Requires legal and IRS changes	Always	Usually
Involves name change for smaller organization	Usually	Usually
"New normal" requires three or more years to develop completely and achieve full buy-in	Usually	Usually

Note: Response range: never, rarely, sometimes, usually, always

Urge to Merge

Church mergers tend to be prompted by a crisis more so than are business mergers. Perhaps the membership in the prospective joining church has dwindled to the point that the church can no longer pay even the basic bills for upkeep on its building. Maybe a long-term pastor has retired and the church can't find someone else who can lead it forward. Maybe a flood, aging roof, or new law requiring fire sprinklers has triggered a large-scale rebuilding effort, causing a struggling church to question whether it has the energy, focus, or resources to tackle a challenge that large. In cases like these—and unlike business mergers—the merger is usually initiated by the smaller organization asking to unite with a larger, healthier congregation. It often involves a major financial challenge already existing in the smaller organization, such as serious debt or threats of foreclosure.

Often a merger is prompted by a stable or stuck church that is dissatisfied with the status quo and wants to break out of the comfortable but ineffective state of affairs. The one exception is the marriage merger. This usually involves a strategic partnership between two strong or stable churches. In such cases the trigger is less of a crisis or dissatisfaction and more of a dream that the two working together can be more effective than each working alone. For marriage mergers, either party initiates the discussion. Financial issues are typically only a minimal factor in such mergers.

In all types of church mergers, the idea is usually proposed as a win for both organizations. It's a win for the kingdom of God, for the witness to the gospel in that particular community, and for the ongoing vision of each local church.

Voting

In most business mergers, voting occurs only in the boardroom. The staff and stockholders rarely participate in the decision to merge with another company. Sometimes they don't even know about it until everything has been decided.

By contrast, churches usually involve many people, and at various levels, in deciding to merge. Church policies differ in terms of who is required to vote on a decision about a merger but many churches initiate a vote, or at least a poll, even when not legally required. Doing so creates opportunity for people to feel like their voice was heard and therefore will create more ownership for the outcome. The vote or poll often becomes a point of remembrance when the adjustments feel painful, especially for the smaller church. For example, you might hear, "Two years ago, after much discussion and prayer, ABC Church voted by 84 percent to join us. You have made many adjustments, some perhaps very uncomfortable. Along the way you may have asked if it's worth it, and today we want to again thank and honor all who came from ABC Church." When it comes to voting on a church merger, consultant Tom Bandy recommends, "Always vote for a vision, never vote for a merger. . . . Merger is just one step toward a larger, bolder, ten-year plan to grow God's mission in the community."[2]

Consultant

Though contracting the services of a consultant is common in the business world, the use of consultants is only slowly being embraced in the church world. A third-party facilitator can be beneficial to the delicate negotiation tensions between two congregations. The facilitator can smooth the way by bringing experienced objective advice that helps guide the merger process. The skillful facilitator helps both congregations to see the realities that the congregations can't or won't see. This person can name the "elephant in the room" that both parties are reluctant to address out of courtesy or fear. The facilitator often becomes the mediator that helps both parties land on resolutions to sticky merger issues. Though mergers have the potential of being a huge win for local churches, there are many landmines to step on along the pathway. It is highly recommended to go down the merger pathway with a skilled guide who knows the terrain.

According to merger specialist David Raymond, "Almost every successful merger has found it essential to use an outside coach or consultant to facilitate the process of merger. An outside party brings both fairness and objectivity to the process, and an experienced consultant can help you avoid mistakes and carry out all of the necessary steps in a timely way."[3]

Personnel Changes

Staff transitions are undoubtedly the stickiest issue associated with a merger, in both the church and business worlds. In churches a change in staff is a delicate issue because of the relationship between staff and congregation and also because Christians want to treat outgoing staff with honor, compassion, and when possible, generosity.

If the merger involves a smaller single-staff church folding into a larger church, what will happen to that staff member, who is typically a pastor? Will Marotti's situation of the pastor wanting to go plant another church is not the norm. More often the pastor is helped to make a transition out of both organizations such as into retirement or into a move to another church in another city. If the smaller church pastor is brought onto the staff with the larger church, it is usually into a new role, not as the senior pastor or co-pastor, as we'll explain more in Chapter Eight on personnel changes (which also addresses the issue of paid and volunteer leaders). Rarely does the smaller church pastor stay on in the role of campus pastor if the merger has a multisite outcome.

The Leadership Network 2011 survey of church mergers indicated that more than 90 percent of pastors continued postmerger in a staff role but very few as the lead pastor or co-pastor. The one exception is the marriage approach to merger, when the joining church pastor might become the senior associate pastor.

More than 90 percent of pastors continued postmerger in a staff role.

Name Change

The vast majority of church mergers involve a name change, as do business mergers. Usually the smaller organization or church takes on the name of the lead company or church. Though the merger itself may occur quickly, the new normal in the merged church usually takes one to three or more years to develop and achieve full buy-in by the group that has had to change the most.

Like all business mergers, any formal church merger also requires legal and IRS changes. Mergers also involve asset transfers—from equipment to properties and buildings. These steps always require a certain degree of financial cost, even if the labor is donated, such as by an attorney or CPA in one and sometimes both of the congregations.

But Not Conflict Free

The biggest finding about mergers from a huge national survey of over ten thousand churches is that merged churches, when compared to their nonmerged counterparts, have greater likelihood of conflict that results in people leaving.[4] In many ways that situation seems predictable: any time you merge two distinct cultures, whether under positive or less-pleasant circumstances, there is a chance of conflict, hurt feelings, overlapping power structures, mixed identities, and so on.

When Will Marotti's younger New Life Church merged with the long-established church, the agreed-on plan was to keep all paid staff from both congregations. Then things turned unexpectedly sour, and many worshipers left from the joining church and from New Life. The exodus also resulted in a loss of more than 20 percent of the income, which led to cuts, first in programs and then staff layoffs. As Will tells in his instructive book, *America's Best Hope*,[5] those were very difficult days. They were draining emotionally and spiritually as well as financially.

If he could go back to that initial "why don't we merge?" discussion, would he do it over again? He would, but he'd approach it with more knowledge. "If we do another merger," he says, "I'll be better prepared for how it works, including any pain and struggle."

He'd also know a bit more about how to define success. "Our standard was that we didn't want to change what's working," he says, "but beyond that, perhaps we didn't map out enough particulars."

Even so, he can now point to many indicators of success. The church has since grown past the merger pains—spiritually, financially, and numerically. New Life helped fund the pastor in the smaller church to launch a new church, and it too is growing. New Life did inherit a beautiful piece of property with great access just off the intersection of two of Connecticut's well-traveled interstate highways. And it retained some great people who love God and want to keep reaching out.

As such, Will wants to keep dreaming big dreams of what God might do. "After all," he explains, "little dreams need no faith. We are to be creative and innovative and to use any legitimate means by all means to transform our community into America's best hope," he says, echoing the title of his book. "We need to continue being open to collaboration and the joining of resources to accomplish God's vision. If God can use me and our ministry to influence many and bring positive transformation to our community, he can use anyone!"

6

WHY MERGERS FAIL

Church mergers are more like merging two family
businesses. Relationships, trust, and communication
are absolutely critical.

—*Response to Leadership Network*
2011 survey of church mergers

Too many mergers fail. In the business world, the majority do.
"Recent studies show the failure rate of mergers is close to 75
percent, and the majority don't produce the expected financial
returns for years after the merger has taken place," a management professor at the University of Pennsylvania's Wharton
School recently wrote.[1]

Most church mergers that fail are motivated more by survival concerns than by vision. Successful mergers are vehicles of
change, not preservers
of the status quo.

The problem is that
the people involved
rarely frame the issue as
one of survival. Some

*Successful mergers are vehicles
of change, not preservers of the
status quo.*

don't even realize that their sights are no higher than defining
success as staying alive for the foreseeable future.

Typical is the failed merger a Michigan pastor told us about.
He framed it as an issue of squatters' rights for the joining
church, which was the older of the two small congregations that
merged. "I was here first," individuals conveyed to him almost as
soon as the formal merger took place, "and so I have more to say
about how things should work out than the other group does,
and our vote counts more."

Yes, both congregations had agreed to merge, signed the necessary documents, and prayed sincerely that God would bless their newly blended church family. But things started going south rather quickly after the lead church, which was a younger congregation that had experienced only leased facilities until they moved into the joining congregation's facility, which hadn't been updated in years.

The backfiring of the merger showed up first in the nursery as a team of young mothers set about painting it in brighter colors and tossing older toys and furniture that they deemed unsafe. They assumed that their energy and enthusiasm would be welcomed by the two grandmothers who had decorated the nursery two decades previously and served as its unchallenged matrons ever since. The next friction point was in the kitchen when the new group brought in their own three-step coffee-maker system, which a connoisseur in their group had refined over the years, and was certain that the church they were merging with would appreciate over their older, simpler approach to the coffee hour. Soon the troubled merger was being challenged at the church boardroom level in tones of "us" and "them."

No one ever voiced or perhaps even thought about the truth that the older joining church saw the merger as little more than an effort to restore a failed status quo. They loved their church, especially their memory of a more vibrant past, and assumed that the new congregation would be their ticket to preserve the parts of their church that they liked best. Like so many churches, they had lost their ability to discern the times and biblically engage their culture in a relevant way.

Meanwhile reality for the younger congregation, as the lead congregation, was that they came to the merger primarily to alleviate crushing financial pressures. They were overstaffed (spending 75 percent of their income on personnel), focused largely on themselves, and excited to get a place to call home for little more than the cost of a cosmetic face-lift.

Although both talked about doing great things for God through the merger, each proceeded to continue with its own agenda, one that was largely unchanged from premerger days, one that didn't have much vision to begin with.

Both churches were focused on institutional survival with an occasional "yea God!" moment from vacation Bible school, youth missions trips, or the coming home of a wayward child. No one was desperate to make a dramatic change.

Had this merger centered on a vote for a vision to grow God's mission in the community, it probably wouldn't have settled for merely continuing the past. Lacking true vision, the merger experienced an initial euphoria followed by a slow unraveling until it imploded.

Too often, that's what happens and the merger fails. In many cases it doesn't need to.

Landmines to Avoid

The challenge of institutional survival versus shared mission and vision for the future is central to every merger's success or failure. But even if the missional dream of reaching the lost, making disciples, training leaders for ministry, and making the community a better place is truly the centerpiece of the merger, there are still several ways it can be derailed. Church mergers can be a fast-track, cost-effective, leap-frog way of multiplying church impact. They can also be a huge distraction and a drain of time, energy, and resources. There are many landmines to step on in the process, and they can be found in three distinct phases.

> *The challenge of institutional survival versus shared mission and vision for the future is central to every merger's success or failure.*

Landmines in the Preliminary Phase

Waiting too long to consider merging. Unfortunately, the vast number of stuck or struggling churches wait too long to even entertain the possibility of a merger. Many well-meaning church leaders will hang on for years with the vague hope that things will somehow turn around miraculously if we "just have faith." Or even worse, many know that change is needed but lack the courage to confront reality. Meanwhile the church declines slowly. The facilities deteriorate through lack of funds and maintenance, and they become more of a liability than an asset. The attendance gets lower as the average age gets higher. The reputation of the church declines as its capacity to do good in the community decreases. Before they realize it, the church has passed a point of no return, in most cases making a merger less appealing to a potential lead church.

As Gary Shockley, executive director of church planting for the United Methodists, told us, "The United Methodist Church has many church facilities that are now worthless and extremely difficult to sell because of deferred maintenance and deferred intervention." Leaders from other denominations have made similar statements.

Lack of clarity on the non-negotiables. Once a church has decided that merging with another church is a possibility, it is important to clearly define what the non-negotiables are even before a merger opportunity presents itself. Church leaders who know why their church exists (their mission), who know what they are trying to accomplish (their vision), who are guided by well-defined values (the way we do church), and have a clear plan for implementing their vision (their strategy) are in the best position to evaluate if a merger makes sense. The more clarity and similarity of the mission, vision, values, and strategy, the easier it is to discern if the proposed merger is a good possibility. It also will make the merger negotiations move forward simpler and faster.

Proceeding with insufficient information. In one merger we heard about, the lead church pastor felt downright misled. The joining church pastor had approached him saying that he'd like to move on and that his church would love to become a campus of the lead church. He said he had thirty people but it turned out there were only four who wanted to be part of the merger. It also turned out that his congregation had a bad reputation in the community, so the incoming lead church was initially viewed as guilty by association. It also turned out that they were only leasing the building where they met. The experience affirms the need for churches to check out each other's story beyond the way one person may be presenting it.

Confusion about models and roles. Once merger discussions begin in earnest, it is important for both parties to correctly define their relationship to one another. As we have indicated throughout this book, mergers are rarely the joining of two equals, even if they describe themselves that way. One church typically leads and the other follows or joins. Often the joining church sees the merger as a marriage and the lead church sees it as a rebirth or adoption. The lead church mistakenly uses marriage

> *Mergers are rarely the joining of two equals, even if they describe themselves that way.*

or partnership language that does not correctly convey the relationship out of fear of offending the joining church.

This lack of clarity about the model each has agreed on can feel like a bait-and-switch scenario later to the joining church and lead to resentment and disillusionment postmerger. The sooner both parties understand who is leading and who is following, the smoother the merger deliberations can proceed. Once they can agree to what kind of merger is being proposed, the quicker they can decide if this merger is desirable. Is this a rebirth, adoption, marriage, reconciliation, or ICU merger?

One helpful way of defining the relationship early in the merger conversation is to look at different models of how two circles might intersect. Figure 6.1 shows those options.

Having unclear or different expectations between the two parties leads to aborted, contentious, or failed mergers. The diagrams

Figure 6.1 Four Ways to Visualize a Church Merger

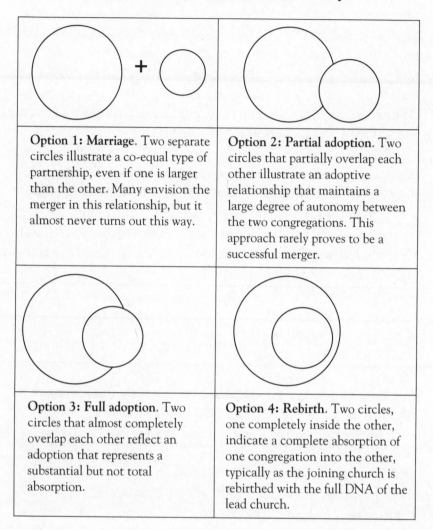

Option 1: Marriage. Two separate circles illustrate a co-equal type of partnership, even if one is larger than the other. Many envision the merger in this relationship, but it almost never turns out this way.

Option 2: Partial adoption. Two circles that partially overlap each other illustrate an adoptive relationship that maintains a large degree of autonomy between the two congregations. This approach rarely proves to be a successful merger.

Option 3: Full adoption. Two circles that almost completely overlap each other reflect an adoption that represents a substantial but not total absorption.

Option 4: Rebirth. Two circles, one completely inside the other, indicate a complete absorption of one congregation into the other, typically as the joining church is rebirthed with the full DNA of the lead church.

shown in Figure 6.1 help clarify the expectations up front and reduce misunderstanding from occurring later in the journey.

It's very important for both churches to discuss and define together which of these four circle diagrams best describes their understanding of the potential merger. If they don't, they might experience what initially happened when a two-hundred-person congregation joined The Chapel in Akron, Ohio, which had an attendance of several thousand. The joining church wrongly felt this was a marriage of equals (option one) rather than an adoption (options two and three) or rebirth (option four). As the church's executive pastor, David Fletcher, told us, "The merger was eventually successfully integrated by both congregations, but by using marriage partnership language out of courtesy and good intentions, we probably caused more hard feelings than necessary with inaccurate expectations that we invited."

Landmines in the Deliberation Phase

Looking back instead of forward. Once two churches have decided that a merger is possible, the merger deliberations can be derailed by focusing on institutional survival or preservation of the past rather than on a shared mission and vision for the future. Even though church leaders may enter into a merger discussion with sincere intentions of a new beginning, often the unconscious but real agenda is to maintain the church without really changing and embracing a new future. They see the infusion of energy and resources as a way to survive rather than to experience a new beginning. Typically, a desire to change will not happen until the pain of not changing is greater than the pain of changing. Successful church mergers occur best when the church knows it needs to change and desires it.

Refusal to release control. The most common landmine occurs when the senior pastor, senior lay leaders, or influential members of the joining church are unable or unwilling to relinquish control of their church. Control issues are usually the most difficult issues to overcome in merger deliberations. Sadly, most struggling churches would rather hold onto the steering wheel of their sinking ship than turn the helm over to an effective leader who knows how to sail the ship. They would rather die than change—and many will do just that.

Minimizing the cultural and doctrinal differences. Another mistake churches make is proceeding with the merger even though the early deliberations revealed that their differences were greater than their similarities. Mergers have the best chance of success when there is at least an 80 percent match in doctrine, philosophy of ministry, and ministry style between the two churches. Some of the typical issues that are extremely difficult to overcome are differing worship styles, different attitudes toward the role of women in the church, opposite approaches to engaging popular culture, accessibility of leaders, and the transfer of assets. The failure to really understand each other's culture is a major cause for postmerger failure. The better each church understands the other's culture, the fewer landmines they will step on.

> *Mergers have the best chance of success when there is at least an 80 percent match in doctrine, philosophy of ministry, and ministry style between the two churches.*

Undercommunicating. Another landmine that occurs during the deliberation stage is poor or insufficient communication to the congregation. The most important step after recommending a merger to your church is to overcommunicate to both congregations the why, the how, and the benefits of merging. Potential benefits of merging might include greater health and vitality as a congregation, an increased number of people who become followers of Christ through the church, more positive name recognition, more culturally relevant ministries, proven best practices, and financial sustainability. When there is an absence of information about the merger, people will fill in the vacuum with incorrect, incomplete, or negative information. Communicating to the congregation is done through FAQs (see examples in the appendixes), timelines in the church bulletin, on the church website, congregational town hall meetings, and multiple meetings with key counterparts from both congregations. Failing to address all the questions and concerns of the church family can result in a failed church vote or great dissatisfaction postmerger.

The Leadership Network 2011 survey of church merg-ers affirmed the sentiment that communication is key in any church merger. "Some people thought the first three months were an 'experiment,'" one survey respondent said. "We merged services at the beginning of summer and the dynamics changed after Labor Day. Some thought things would 'get back to nor-mal.' Clearly, that wasn't going to happen!"

One of the lead churches surveyed expressed that they wished they had handled communication for the joining church. "What we learned is that the leadership of the [joining] church didn't communicate very well—they didn't know how," this church said. "A lot of information was fuzzy and confusing for the [joining] church."

The pastor of a church in Colorado that experienced a suc-cessful merger underscored the importance of overcommunicat-ing. His staff and the joining church staff collaboratively worked hard to give clear and unified communication during the merger process. Doing so "prevented an 'us and them' dynamic from emerging," the pastor said. He looks back at those efforts as one of the biggest positive steps forward during the first three months after the merger.

Landmines in the Postmerger Phase

Underestimating the pain in the transition. As change management specialist William Bridges states:

> It isn't the changes that do you in, it's the transitions. They aren't the same thing.
>
> **Change** is situational: the move to a new site, the retirement of the founder, the reorganization of the roles on the team, the revisions to the pension plan.
>
> **Transition,** on the other hand, is psychological; it is a three-phase process that people go through as they internalize and

come to terms with the details of the new situation that the change brings about.[2]

William Bridges' three-phase process starts with an *ending*, and leaders need to clarify exactly what is ending and what is not. Next comes a disorienting sort of "nowhere" that he calls *the neutral zone*. Jim likes to describe this to his merger clients as the "tunnel of chaos." Then comes the new *beginning*. If people don't deal with each of these phases, the change will be "just a rearrangement of the furniture," William Bridges says, with the outcome that "it didn't work."[3]

Change is an event, something that happens. Transition is the emotional and psychological processing of the change. Making the decision to merge is not easy, but it is the transition that determines the ultimate outcome. Transition is about the journey and how to get there. One of the reasons that mergers unravel is that not enough attention is paid to the transition process.

> *Change is an event, something that happens. Transition is the emotional and psychological processing of the change.*

Overpromising and underdelivering. The postmerger integration is the final and most crucial phase in successful church mergers. The biggest mistakes churches make after the merger has been approved are in the integration and follow-through postmerger. Often so much time and energy is focused on getting the merger accomplished that less attention is given to the postmerger integration. There is a tendency to overpromise the benefits of a merger during the deliberation stage and then underdeliver the results during the postmerger integration stage.

Many church mergers get off to a bad start because of a failure to integrate operations and systems quickly. The first three months are critical to successful integration. The merged church enters a zone of chaos as people move from the familiar and comfortable way of doing things to an unfamiliar and uncertain way of functioning. As soon as the merger is approved, the new chapter needs to begin *immediately*. New signs, systems, and procedures must be in place and functioning as soon as possible, preferably the following week.

Unclear organizational structure. Parallel to this mistake is the landmine of starting the postmerger integration with undefined leadership and unclear reporting structures. On the day after the merger is approved, it has to be clear to everyone in the church—staff, lay leaders, church members, and attendees—who's in charge here and where do I fit on the church organizational chart? Confusion here will breed anger and frustration.

From a Consultant's Perspective

Also consider this top-ten list from Tom Bandy, a noted church consultant, and author of several titles including *Coaching Change* and *95 Questions to Shape the Future of Your Church*. In a blog he identifies pitfalls to consider carefully and avoid in a potential merger:

1. The merger was never really driven by a vision. Despite the rhetoric of staff and members, the *real* motivation for the merger is to solve an *institutional problem* that is somehow beyond the power of the individual churches to resolve. The motivation is not really aimed to solve a *mission challenge* that is beyond the individual churches to achieve.

2. The merger cannot eliminate "sacred cows" (properties, programs, technologies, or people). Leaders are not able to measure the real productivity of traditional ministries for the changing mission field. Income and energy continue to be sidetracked away from the agenda of God's purpose to redeem the world.

3. The merger conversation fails to include the public. Leaders and members are prayerful; boards meet; members converse; but

the churches do not really involve the diverse micro-cultures in the mission field to shape the new vision that God is revealing. The merged church is still too homogeneous, and fails to mirror the demographic diversity of the community.

4. The "signature ministries" fail to respect one another. Most churches will bring to a merger some major outreach ministry in which they invest significant money and leadership energy. These "signature ministries" have enjoyed considerable authority in the church, and too often become competitive for space, budget, and prestige.

5. There are "hidden controllers" who are unable to surrender ego or self-interest to the larger purposes of God. "Controllers" are dysfunctional people who want to shape the church around personal lifestyle, and are unwilling to shape personal lifestyle around the mission. Their intimidating personalities or personal neediness sidetracks the church from its higher purpose.

6. Staff and core leaders fail to integrate as a team. They fail to hold one another accountable for mission attitude, high integrity, skills competency, and teamwork. It only takes one staff person to prioritize [his or her] program silo, personal power, or salary package over the needs of the whole church to sabotage trust.

7. The organizational model fails to become a streamlined, team-based, mission-driven structure. Instead, bureaucracies in each church that are already too large are integrated by artificial representation to form an even larger and more unwieldy board and committee structure. Decision making slows down and innovation becomes secondary to program protection.

8. The newly merged church starts too timidly. Leaders and members are too "soft-hearted" and "merciful" around one another. They fail to assertively embed a new DNA, and worry too much about maintaining harmony. The inevitable loss of some members unduly terrifies them.

9. The newly merged church is drawn down to the lowest common denominator of excellence, rather than rise up to the highest standard of expectation. Each church brings strengths and weaknesses to the merger, but the newly merged church waits too long for weak leaders to step up and excellent leaders become too frustrated.

10. A middle judicatory (parent denomination) meddles in the newly merged church, imposing policies and procedures that sidetrack the newly formed community of faith from mission to polity. Usually this involves restrictions about staffing, volunteer deployment, ideology, or credentialing.[4]

The bottom line, according to Tom Bandy, is that *leaders never ask the participating congregations to commit to a merger.* They ask faithful Christians to *commit to a large, bolder, biblical vision.* The merger is only one step in a multiyear plan to expand God's mission through the creation of a new organizational entity.

Insights from the Business World

Much business literature is devoted to the topic of mergers and acquisitions. One book cites four reasons for failure,[5] each of which applies to the church world:

- *Cost.* Paying too much. The financial costs may make the merger prohibitive. Be thorough in determining all costs and hidden liabilities. For an excellent detailed model, see the FAQs from Ginghamsburg Church in Appendix D.
- *DNA.* Poor strategic fit. Proceeding with a merger when the DNA match is less than 80 percent is a recipe for disaster.
- *Process.* Incomplete or haphazard due diligence. Be sure all issues are addressed before agreeing to a merger. See Chapter Twelve for a list of all the issues and especially Chapter Seven for all the legal matters related to a merger.

- *Integration.* Ineffective integration is essential. In business parlance, it's much easier to do a deal than to implement it. As authors Galpin and Herndon say, "The key to successful integration is a systematic, thorough, and expedient process."[6] As in the business world, it's less likely to fail if it moves fairly quickly. "Today the businesses must be merged as quickly as possible—often within six to twelve months after the close."[7]

We agree with these cautions. In Chapter Twelve we'll describe twenty-five crucial issues to work through, any of which could lead to a failed church merger. According to the Leadership Network 2011 survey of church mergers, the most common area of failure is culture clash.

7

FINANCIAL AND LEGAL ASPECTS OF A MERGER

"Robert, would you please come downstairs to the conference room?" That intercom request came on a January 2006 morning. Robert Bowman, at the time associate pastor for missions and ministries at Central Baptist Bearden in midtown Knoxville, Tennessee, entered the conference room and saw his senior pastor, his church administrator, and two other men he knew well. One was the local Baptist Association director and the other was a retired pastor serving as interim pastor of a Baptist church located four miles away. Both were members of Central Baptist Bearden.

Robert was well aware of the nearby Baptist church. The two guests shared with Robert how they had recently counseled the dwindling congregation to formally close its doors. The church had been around for more than fifty years, many of them vibrant years with over three hundred in regular attendance. Yet the Sunday before, there had been fewer than thirty people present.

Their question was, "Would Central Baptist be interested in acquiring this facility?" Robert's first thought was an enthusiastic "Yes!" Ideas for its use began racing through his head.

But there were also some liabilities. The church had a debt of about $310,000, which meant the entire Central Baptist congregation would need to vote on it. It also turned out that the small and declining congregation was not unanimous in its desire to sell its assets. Some wanted to formally merge with Central Baptist, others wanted help in coming back to health, and others wanted their church to join Central Baptist as a multisite worshipping church.

During the next three months, Robert led a task force that explored all angles of the opportunity. When they presented their recommendation to the membership of Central Baptist, it gave a unanimous vote to acquire the facility.

Meanwhile, Robert developed a good relationship with the trustees of the other church. He attended their last worship service as a congregation on Easter 2006. Two of the three trustees ended up joining Central Baptist.

The outcome has been a huge success in Robert's view. "It wasn't a pure merger," he explains, "because the congregation was too far gone." But Central Baptist did pay off the church's debt and purchase its facilities. This involved paying for an appraiser. Central Baptist was fortunate to have an attorney in the church who was able to handle the appropriate forms required by the state and other red tape issues. The sale also involved moral and ethical dimensions because the joining church asked Central Baptist, as the lead church, to make verbal agreements that the facility would be used as a church or for other ministry purposes, thus not reselling it to a developer or other for-profit buyer.

Central Baptist continued to remain as a single-site church in terms of worship at its original facility. The added location, rebranded as a missional venture of Central Baptist, became an immediate boon to three of Central Baptist's large ministries, all of which needed additional space. One was a Christian drama troupe founded by members of Central Baptist, who enjoyed having access to the newly acquired facility's platform stage, storage space, and permanent rehearsal space. A second was a fully developed HIV/AIDS ministry that had been birthed within Central Baptist and was delighted to have office space, meeting rooms for support groups, and even a sanctuary for small funerals. The third ministry was Imani Community Church that had begun in 2003 serving African immigrants.

Other resident partners included a new Anglican congregation and the regional offices for a ministry to the disabled. In addition, there are nonresident users as space permits, including a ministry that speaks out against child sexual abuse, a ministry focused on life transformation of single moms, and a men's Bible study.

During 2010 the building was paid off and became self-supporting. Currently all available space is being used and there is even a waiting list with new requests. "God has done so much more than even we imagined or asked," Robert says.

Time for Attorneys

Lots of questions need to be covered when a merger occurs. Just a few of the legal questions include the following:

- Who has the legal authority to approve the merger and what happens if some of the members of the church aren't on board with what's going on?

- Who owns what and how does the lead church know what it's receiving?

- Who needs to be told what and when? Is there a certain order of events that should be followed?

- What rights do the people have who funded purchases of the land, facilities, and other assets of the joining church?

- What are the obligations of board members from the lead church and the joining church?

- How should moral obligations be handled, such as an earlier promise to Susie, the longtime secretary of the joining church, whose leaders had verbally promised that the church would take care of her in her retirement?

- Does the joining church need title insurance? For example, in one case a board member appeared after a merger and said, "I wasn't told about the merger, and I would have voted 'no,' so I'm finding a lawyer to have the transaction voided."

- In short, how can the merger be done legally, morally, and ethically?

The answers to most of these questions are found generally in the Bible and specifically in each church's governance documents, such as its articles of incorporation, constitution, and bylaws, as well as in the laws of the state and country of the merging churches.

There are many legal issues involved in a church merger. Many churches retain legal counsel to walk them through the intricacies of the merger process—and in most cases; it's wisest for all parties to involve legal representation. Obviously, fees may vary depending on the attorney but generally it is a small price to pay to ensure that all the legal bases are covered. One attorney whose firm specializes in churches and has dealt with hundreds of church mergers nationwide over the years is David Middlebrook of Church Law Group (www.churchlawgroup.com). His law practice focuses on religious nonprofit organizations. He coauthored *Nonprofit Law for Religious Organizations: Essential Questions and Answers*,[1] which provides guidance, direction, and clarification of legal and tax laws affecting churches and other religious organizations.

Three Ways to Merge

David suggests there are three options for approaching a merger, recommending the third as the preferred approach. His firm has also reviewed the following text for legal accuracy.

Option One: Merger

Legally speaking, a merger in the United States is a formal and legal procedure in which articles of merger are filed with the secretary of state. The process involves a merging entity (the joining church) and a surviving entity (the lead church). In a merger, the surviving entity assumes all of the assets and liabilities of the merging entity.

- *Pro:* Sometimes it's the only available method for churches to come together, such as if the joining church has an existing loan, lawsuit, or other outstanding obligation.
- *Con:* In this approach, the merger works much like a marriage and the lead church must assume all liabilities, even those that are unknown. Further, this approach can take more time than the other options to accomplish if it involves third parties, such as working with a lender to ensure that a loan passes to the surviving entity. Finally, it can be more expensive in attorney fees due to complications associated with working through third parties.

Option Two: Asset Purchase and Dissolution

In this option, which is something like a garage sale, one corporation (the lead church) purchases the assets of another corporation (the joining church). By purchasing the assets, the goal is that the lead church provides the joining church with enough funding to pay out its existing financial liabilities. After all assets have been purchased, the joining church is then formally dissolved by filing articles of dissolution through the secretary of state's office or filing a similar document with the appropriate state office, depending on the state in which the joining church is located.

This option is appropriate in situations in which there are outstanding debts or liabilities, such as a lease or loan that must be addressed before the dying entity can be dissolved.

- *Pro:* Legally speaking, this approach is a better option than a pure merger. It allows the joining church to pay off its known liabilities while protecting the lead church from assuming unknown liabilities, such as perhaps the later discovery that the joining church's building is atop a sinkhole or toxic waste dump, or that a children's minister had an inappropriate relationship with a youth member ten years ago that was never reported and which the current leaders of the joining church had forgotten or did not know about.

- *Con:* Many churches do not like this idea simply because the term sounds "too corporate." Also the lead church, as the purchasing corporation, must come up with adequate cash to purchase all assets of the joining church. Plus this option usually involves an attorney and thus in many cases a legal fee will be incurred.

Option Three: Donation and Dissolution

In this option, one corporation (the joining church) donates all its assets to another corporation (the lead church). There is no purchase of assets involved. Rather, the lead church accepts all of the assets of the joining church just as it would accept any other donation from any other donor. The donating corporation then formally dissolves by filing articles of dissolution with the secretary of state or filing a similar document with the appropriate state office, depending on the state. This process works because the Internal Revenue Service (IRS) allows a nonprofit organization to make donations to another tax-exempt organization at any time and mandates such an act on the dissolution of a nonprofit corporation.

As with option two, the joining church is formally dissolved after all assets have been transferred by filing articles of dissolution with the secretary of state. This approach avoids liability issues by not leaving an empty corporate shell in existence that becomes linked to the name of the lead church. An entity still in existence can be sued even if it is no longer functioning.

- *Pro:* This is the cleanest, most straightforward, and quickest method of combining two organizations. Little if any liability is involved because only the assets of the donating corporation are being transferred. Liabilities, whether hidden or public, are not transferred. Typically, all that is needed to formalize the arrangement is a vote of the respective churches' memberships (if such voting rights exist) or corporate resolutions to be signed by the respective boards of directors.

- *Con:* It can be somewhat rare for a church to be completely without debt or with such assets on hand that it can pay off any remaining liabilities without the need for assistance from the lead church. Therefore, this is not always an option for many churches.

Additional Issues to Consider

David Middlebrook also affirms the importance of dealing with five other matters, advising that legal counsel be brought in as needed:

Documents: Prior to the merger, a study should be made of the joining church's corporate documents to determine how they govern the dissolution process and whether they contain any potentially conflicting statements. Do they identify who has the power to authorize dissolution? Are there any reversionary clauses, such as if the entity ceases to exist, all remaining assets revert back to a denomination or other organization? Depending on what is found, the joining church may need to amend its corporate documents before it can merge, sell, or donate its assets.

Employees: What will happen to the employees of the joining church? In most cases, all employees who remain employees of the surviving entity will need to re-sign employment agreements. Any employees who will have access to children may need to have new background checks run and perhaps other verifications made.

Real property: All land, buildings, and similar physical assets need to be identified and included in the merger. It is amazing how many churches have all but forgotten unused acreage that someone gave the church long ago for the church's youth group to use for camping. Also, if a church is part of a denomination, it may need to seek denominational approval and determine whether the church property is owned by the denomination before proceeding. However, if the joining church was leasing its space, someone will need to contact the landlord to inquire as to whether or not the landlord would be willing to assign the lease to or renegotiate with the lead church—if the lead church wants to continue to use that space as opposed to strictly purchasing or accepting the donated assets. If the lead church does not want to continue using the leased space, the remaining term of the lease should be addressed. Commercial landlords are usually not keen on the idea of their tenants skipping a lease years before it is scheduled to finish, and if a pastor or trustee of the joining church signed a personal guarantee on that lease, the landlord could potentially come against them personally for the amounts of any outstanding rent payments owed for the remainder of the contracted lease term.

Personal property: Of course the larger issues regarding personal properties will need to be addressed. Any items that are currently financed or under lease, such as copy machines, will need to be paid off, returned to the vendor, or assigned (if possible) to the lead church. Personal property that is titled, such as vans or trailers, will need to be collected and transferred over to the lead church. However, the joining church will also need to appoint one or more individuals to go through all of the joining church's assets to take an inventory. How many chairs does the joining church own? Computers? Desks? Trash cans? Nursery beds? Hymnals? What about the valuable but no-longer-used collection of theatrical spotlights that have been stored in Deacon Charlie's garage for the last several years after the church didn't have enough budget or people to continue its big dramatic productions? The lead church will need to obtain such an inventory so that it can be fully aware of exactly what it is obtaining.

Restricted gifts: Bequests made over the years to the joining church will also have to be dealt with. The leadership should find out what assets, if any, were accepted under restricted circumstances. Perhaps the former organist had willed money to the church for the specific purpose of a financial endowment designed to maintain the pipe organ. The money has been in the bank for thirty years now, gaining in size because minimal repairs have been needed on the organ. Now for the merger, the organ will be sold. The lead church does not have a pipe organ, nor any plans to buy one. What happens to this financial endowment? Generally, these types of funds cannot be assumed by the lead church without written permission from all of the donors who contributed to such a fund. Does the joining church have all of its records? In some cases, gifts made to the joining church may revert back to the donor or to another heir if the gift is not treated in accordance with certain requirements that may have been placed on the initial gift by the donor. It is critical to communicate with congregants so that gifts to the church find a new home that is suitable to the giver and nothing is lost in the transition.

Dollars Involved in a Merger

Legal fees can be as low as nothing, if the church has access to an attorney with the appropriate specialty and expertise, as in the case of the Central Baptist story at the beginning of this chapter. David Middlebrook has known of mergers that have cost less than $1,000 in legal fees (including filing fees to dissolve the joining church) to as much as $50,000 in cases with major complications, such as when there is dissention among the members of the joining church, with some of the opposing members feeling so strongly against the merger that they intentionally wreak havoc for those trying to facilitate the merger; or in scenarios involving lots of property or large sums of money, such as when the joining church has large debt that must be transferred in accordance with the requirements of the lender; or in scenarios when the joining church has a large number of restricted gifts that must be appropriately transferred and possibly returned to the original donors.

According to the Leadership Network 2011 survey of church mergers, the costs to complete a merger are often surprisingly low. Predictably, merger costs vary by church size, but generally it's very modest. Average costs for the merger and twelve subsequent months are as follows:

- $18,000 for churches whose combined attendances are 25–199
- $73,000 for attendances of 200–999
- $635,000 for attendance of 1,000–1,999
- $469,000 for attendance 2,000–14,000

Categories for expenses during the merger and subsequent twelve months included debt payment, facility renovations including new technology and equipment, attorney and legal fees, mortgage or rent, honoring existing commitments such as monthly support for a missionary, severance for staff or supported missionaries, publicity and branding (signage, stationary, website, etc.), and ongoing staff salaries. More than one church reported something like, "It cost very little because the merging church had some assets" or "The only costs were for staff because the joining church had sufficient assets to cover their remaining obligations."

Avoiding a Real Estate Scramble

In Chapter Three we warned against the motive of real estate greed. Mergers involve finances, and sometimes property needs to be sold, but deception—including the appearance of deception—should never be a part of a merger plan. Although every lead church postmerger needs to have the freedom to manage its assets to fulfill its mission and be good stewards of their resources, it needs to be forthright in its intentions concerning inherited facilities. Even when the lead church genuinely intends to keep inherited facilities, the financial realities may dictate otherwise. One simple way to preclude a real estate misunderstanding is to include a timeline requirement such as "not sell for at least two years." Another approach is to add one or more elders from the joining church to the lead church's board, knowing that they will be appropriately protective of their former facility, for the first few years at least.

Escape Clause

In an era of prenuptial agreements and let's-live-together-before-we-marry arrangements, should there be an escape clause for churches entering into a merger? We advise against it. Instead of a trial run, go more slowly, give it time, and build more trust. Perhaps enter into one or more joint ventures between the churches as a way to test compatibility toward a possible complete merger in the future.

The very day after we started this section on an escape clause, a church leader asked Jim about the wisdom of it because his church of two hundred and a smaller congregation of 120 are thinking about a merger but both parties have hesitations. As one way to investigate the possibility of merging in the future, they are looking toward sharing the same facility as two separate congregations. Jim affirmed the wisdom of meeting their immediate needs by sharing an affordable facility that allows them the opportunity to explore the merger possibility. That way they can wait to be certain that the merger is God's leading.

8

PERSONNEL CHANGES

An essential issue—and an emotional one at that—for churches to explore as they talk together about a merger is what will happen to the pastor, any staff, the existing board, and the primary committees of the joining church. Every church has key lay leaders serving in official roles and almost every church has someone on a payroll, even if only part time. The larger the church, the more paid staff to deal with in most cases. The most common roles to work through are that of pastor, secretary or equivalent, youth worker, and custodian.

Frank Rondon is a good example of a positive transition in which two lead pastors remained together in one church. Frank, as the joining church pastor, became the associate pastor.

The sequence began when Frank's denomination assigned him to a church that was once thriving but had gone through some rough times under the previous pastor. Frank could not reverse the decline or start a new growth momentum. The church even had to sell its building and become portable.

One day Frank was chatting with a fellow Assemblies of God pastor whose church was about ten minutes away. That man, who was seventy and thinking about retirement, said to Frank, who was thirty-five, "I'm looking for a younger leader like you."

This initial conversation led to a merger in which Frank's congregation of 75 to 100 people, whose ages averaged about forty years old, joined Lowell Assembly of God in Tewksbury, Massachusetts, a congregation with attendance of about 125 and whose people averaged about sixty years old.

As if a divine confirmation occurred, two weeks after the merger, the facility Frank's congregation had been renting was abruptly closed and demolished!

Even with the merger of two very different generations, Frank's church didn't lose a single person due to the merger. To him this was another confirmation because of what he had read in business books about mergers. "They all would predict that our merger won't work. The absorbed organization will die." But it didn't. "We relied on the Holy Spirit, not a business book," he says. "Our merger caused everything to increase—attendance, conversions, community impact, and even openness to change among the people of the lead church."

Frank came in as an associate pastor and remains in that role, serving under the long-standing senior pastor. He preaches occasionally, teaches the adult Sunday school, and generally helps Lowell Assembly of God to transition to "new wineskins" in worship style and culture.

Frank considered that the cost required for the merger "tested character and motives, humility, a kingdom mentality, and a long-term view of ministry," as he describes them. Not everything worked the way he thought it would, but overall he realizes that "the work I put into the congregation before the merger will not go to waste," Frank commented as he looked back on the merger at the one-year mark. "It takes a humble leader to see everything he has worked for be absorbed by the lead church, but the people I brought still look to me as one of their pastors, and the bottom line is that everything was gained for the kingdom of God."

Senior Pastor

The most visible and delicate staff role to discuss in a merger transition is that of pastor. "What will happen to our pastor?" is also one of the first questions to address in the merger conversation. We see four possible pathways.

No Pastor

Only about 30 percent of churches going into a merger do so without pastors in both of the churches, according to the Leadership Network 2011 survey of church mergers. A good example is Chelsea Community Church, located in a suburb of Birmingham, Alabama. The church of almost three hundred people was growing and looking for larger facilities. One of its members had a friend who attended another church in town—one that no longer had a pastor and was thinking about shutting down after 102 years of ministry. Those two friends made appropriate introductions and soon Greg Davis, the pastor of Chelsea Community Church, was talking with two elders of the other church.

The conversations were very frank. "The community sees your church as a dead or dying duck," Greg told the men. "We need to completely rebirth it." This was painful for them to hear because they realized their congregation would lose its identify. Greg invited them to extend the conversation to the rest of the congregation: "You might not even like what we're doing," he said, observing that his congregation was mostly young and worshipped in a contemporary style, and the other church was mostly older people and worshipped in a more traditional style. "Why don't you shut down for a month, come worship with us, and see what you think?"

The struggling church did just that. At that point, Greg started meeting with their thirty-five people, sharing his heart and vision. "The message will be the same, but the methods have to change. I don't want to merge, only two months later for us to be tearing out walls and for you to be upset." He made it clear that if they became part of Chelsea Community Church, they'd change this, remove that from the facility, and continue to target young couples, not their age group. "Our doctrine may be very similar but we're going to be a completely different church," he said.

The church agreed to everything he laid out. Likewise the church's denomination, Church of God Anderson, was willing to release the facility to the interdenominational Chelsea Community Church. With a lot of volunteer work, the church facility experienced a complete face-lift. "I've been doing church ministry for thirty years and have never seen unity like this," Greg says, "and the transformation has ignited a revival." Even some of the people who used to attend that church have come back. The week we interviewed him in 2011, Chelsea Community Church had seen five hundred people in worship the previous Sunday.

As Greg has looked for an additional staff person, who did he find but one of the previous pastors of that church! He was the final pastor at that church, someone who had tried to bring about change and it hadn't been received very well. He had left a year and a half before the merger officially occurred in March 2009. Now people from both congregations have received him well.

In the first year of the merger four families left. One wanted a smaller church, one felt Chelsea's style was too casual, one didn't like something else about the new style, and one moved away. No one left over the merger. Indeed the transition slogan, "putting a new face on history," has turned out to do just that.

Pastor Departs After Merger Is Approved

Sometimes there is no staff position available with the lead church. Other times the joining pastor is retiring or desires a ministry or career change and is not interested in staying post-merger. Sometimes the joining pastor is financially supported in a new ministry endeavor by the lead church.

Regardless of the various reasons for not staying, the pastor's departure is a delicate situation that needs to be handled well. When a pastor decides not to remain, a congregation can feel a sense of rejection from its "beloved" pastor, and good will toward him can turn sour. Resentment can also build toward the lead church if it does retain the pastor in his position.

In all of these situations it is wise to offer a generous severance package and a happy farewell to the departing pastor.

Pastors Become Co-Pastors

This rarely occurs and for good reason: they rarely succeed in terms of the church making more disciples or becoming more outwardly focused. When a co-pastor merger does occur in a church merger, it is often part of a succession plan for one of the pastors. Most often co-pastorates tend to happen in smaller churches, compounding the financial problems the churches were facing as they went into the merger. Even if the finances were not problematic, we still do not recommend this option for mergers, and have not seen a healthy, growing model of co-pastors from merged churches. (We have seen the rare successful co-pastorate that was unrelated to a merger, however.)

It doesn't work, we suspect, because it's too hard for two different church cultures to come together under the umbrella of sharing the best of both worlds and arbitrated by two people who are trying to be equal with each other.

Pastor Becomes Staff at the Lead Church

This is the most common option, even if it lasts only a season, in order to allow the joining church's pastor to depart graciously and it invites a smoother transition. Such arrangements can be spelled out as part of the merger negotiations. For example, the lead church can say, "Both congregations will understand that you'll be an associate pastor with us up to the decision to merge, then we will reposition you somewhere else on our team or release you with a generous severance package."

Sometimes the merger arrangements envision more than a transitional role for the pastor from the joining church. In multisite mergers, the pastor of the joining church rarely assumes the campus pastor role; most are redeployed somewhere else on the staff team. The most common roles we hear about are executive pastor, visitation pastor, small-groups pastor, adult ministries pastor, or missions pastor. The most important success factor is that it be a good fit for the person's strengths and ministry passions.

Gary Foran is an excellent example of a transition that proved to be a better fit than senior pastoring. His self-supporting Detroit church of about 130 people, including eight small groups, merged with a church of about three hundred. The lead church pastor had known Gary well enough before the merger to recognize that Gary had a passion for and strength in developing community through small groups—something that had been missing in the larger church.

"It was a match easily made," Gary told us. "I had offered to join their team working with small groups," he says. "I loved building small groups and the other pastor—a friend—was someone I could follow." Gary then stayed on staff of the larger church for the next twelve years, the first nine of which were helping people connect and grow deeper through small-group community. "It was more successful than even we imagined," he says.

It is not easy to give up the authority and privileges of the senior pastor position and submit and adjust to a lesser role in the lead church. It means you are no longer the primary preacher or the one in charge. Failure to navigate this transition well can result in strained relationships and even a premature forced departure.

Here is some advice that Jim often gives to senior pastors who are transitioning into a new role at the lead church, written as an e-mail he's used:

Pat,

You have successfully navigated a very important milestone in your journey and transitioned [NAME OF JOINING

CHURCH] into its next chapter. You finished well and are well positioned for the future. Yea God!

Here are a few suggestions on how to navigate the next few months in your new role in the merged church:

- Look forward, not backward.

- Keep a low profile with your former congregation, allowing them to bond with other spiritual leaders in the church.
- Don't allow yourself to be a "dump bucket" for disgruntled individuals from your former congregation.
- Be a servant—ask often, "How can I serve you?"
- Be a team player—make yourself invaluable.
- Live within your budget, don't be late to staff and church meetings, maintain expected office hours, and otherwise work hard to fit into the culture of the church you've joined.
- Don't consistently be the first person to offer an opinion.
- Stay positive and take the high road.
- Lean into your gifts and passions.
- Maintain good friendships both outside and inside the church.
- Call me (or a colleague who has no dog in the fight) when you need to unload or process.

I am proud of you and excited for your new chapter. The adventure continues. Keep in touch.

Transitions for Boards

Every church has boards and committees of lay leaders. They have various names according to denominational polity and tradition—elders, deacons, trustees, and so on. Often they are the most influential stakeholders who will make a big difference in the ultimate outcome of a merger.

What happens to them in a merger? Usually the boards and committees of the joining church are dissolved after the merger is approved. Often postmerger some of these lay leaders from the dissolved boards and committees are invited to join the board or committees of the lead church. Their expertise, maturity, and support during the merger process make them valuable players in the delicate postmerger integration stage. Their wisdom, relational connections in the community, and other leadership skills are often some of the most significant benefits that the joining church brings into the merger!

Their wisdom, relational connections, . . . and other . . . skills are often some of the most significant benefits that the joining church brings into the merger!

General Advice for Staff Transitions

- Avoid promises such as "We'll keep all staff and board members." Numerous people told us that they wish they hadn't made the promise because then if staff didn't fit the new culture of the merged church, it was more difficult to help them move to a different place of employment. Promises like that also invite people to take sides: "You didn't keep your promise" or "That's yet another change and loss for us."

- Retain any staff that are genuinely needed and can be afforded.

- Offer generous severance packages relative to how long they've served.

- Be gentle, affirming, and clear.

In addition to the pastor, board, and staff, the other stakeholders in the church also need guidance and coaching through each phase of a merger. They include the lay leaders, volunteers, regular attenders, and those members who participate infrequently or not at all. Each has different needs and issues to be thoughtfully addressed. Each requires a different level of information, communicated in various ways at different times through different channels and formats. Each one will have different access points to the decision-making process, but all will require sensitivity and help in emotionally processing the decision and making the transition. Their transition issues will be further further in Chapter Thirteen, "Managing Pain and Change."

Part Three

YOUR NEXT STEPS

9

DETERMINING WHETHER YOUR CHURCH IS A GOOD MERGER CANDIDATE

As we mentioned previously, 2 percent of US Protestant churches have been part of a merger in the last two years and another 5 percent say they have talked about merging in the next two years, according to Leadership Network research. This means there are fifteen thousand potential merger partners out there—5 percent of three hundred thousand US Protestant churches. If so, which of those might want to merge with you?

As you explore the options, here are the three exploratory questions we introduced in Chapter Two that frame the merger conversation. They will help you determine if your church should even entertain a merger possibility:

- Could we accomplish more together than separate?
- Would our community be better served together?
- Could the kingdom of God be further extended by our merger?

In Chapter Twelve we provide a more detailed self-assessment tool to determine if your church is merger ready, but here are some guidelines for determining if your church is a viable candidate for merging.

Lead Churches

If you're a potential lead church, then the candidates could include many types of joining churches.

Stable and Perhaps Even Strong Churches That Are Dissatisfied with Their Present Status Quo

We were very intentional in choosing the church marriage merger account of Arizona pastor Justin Anderson as one of the first examples in this book. His approach, one that seems to have potential for huge fruitfulness, is akin to the hundredfold crop that comes from seed planted in good soil as Jesus described in Matthew 13:8.

Justin was founding pastor of the dynamic and growing Praxis Church near the campus of Arizona State University. It had grown in attendance to twelve hundred meeting in two locations. Then it merged with the older and more stable East Valley Bible Church in the suburbs of Phoenix, a church that was even larger in attendance. Both congregations were healthy, though at different life stages. Their pastors had a long personal relationship with each other. The merged church took the name Redemption Church.

Why then did they merge? The primary reason was to maximize their strengths in order to multiply congregations across Arizona. They combined the resources, talents, and gifts of each church with a vision, as their website describes, to saturate the state of Arizona with Gospel-centered, Reformed, Missional churches through Missions and church plants.[1]

Young Church Plants

One pastor recently told us, "I heard recently about a two-year-old church plant that just couldn't make it and dissolved. Before they shut everything down, I wish we could have heard their story, and they our story. We might have found a way to work together to continue what they had started."

For another church, that's just what happened. Austin New Church in Austin, Texas, where Brandon Hatmaker is pastor, experienced three mergers in its first three years of life. All were recent church plants like Austin New Church. One was dissolving, one had a similar vision and sought to partner beyond their walls, and one simply did not want to continue into the future the way things were. Each had at least one paid staff member. Brandon already had a relationship with each church and knew the staff members' strengths and likely fit at Austin New Church. For each he found a creative funding method for bringing the church planter and the young church into the fold of Austin New Church.

Established Churches That Are Struggling

Dan Kimball, author of *They Like Jesus but Not the Church*,[2] is pastor of Vintage Faith Church, a nondenominational congregation in Santa Cruz, California. The church had started with a Sunday night worship gathering but Dan realized fast that it needed an additional Sunday morning service, mainly because of young families with children. He and others began searching locally for a place to meet, approached a Presbyterian church whose attendance was small and declining, and asked if they could rent space from them. The Presbyterian Church, mostly elderly people, could worship at 9 AM and Vintage Faith could start an 11AM. "Their leaders knew who we were as we are in a fairly small town," Dan says, "and out of their mission-oriented heart—they were founded in 1889 with very mission-minded focus that continued as part of their DNA—they offered to allow us to meet there at no cost."

Vintage Faith moved its 7 PM gathering to the building and also launched an 11 AM service. Over time, the Presbyterian church asked Dan to teach at its 9 AM service, keeping the organist and Presbyterian format. "We got along so well and shared the same vision to reach our town, that after a year we discussed becoming one church which we eventually did," Dan explains. "We took time to get to know each other, build trust, ask a lot of questions, meet with the Presbytery leaders before we formally became one church." After two years of serving together, including months and months of prayer, discussion, and many meetings, the churches decided to partner together longer term. When that happened in 2008, First Presbyterian Church simply changed its name to Vintage Faith Church. The staff members from both churches joined together as one staff.

Vintage Faith also took on the Presbyterian church's financial responsibilities. The Presbyterian church was overspending $35,000 more than its offerings and living off its fast-dwindling savings. After the merger, Vintage Faith also spent money on building improvements and opening a seven-day-a-week coffeehouse and music venue for local college students in the church building.

Some fallout is always predictable in a merger and about half the Presbyterian church ended up leaving because of the changes Vintage Faith brought to the teaching, worship, and other emphases. "We all did our absolute best to communicate and explain, but some couldn't accept the changes and went to another traditional church in our town," Dan says. But those who stayed became extremely active and served in ministries. One woman who was part of the Presbyterian church for over fifty years comes every Sunday to the 7 PM service and sits in the front row. "She beams and is thrilled seeing her church now filled with young people," Dan reports. Indeed there have been many discussions that imagine aloud how Jesus is pleased with the stewardship of the building, which previously was barely used during the week and is now completely active. "We even gutted the fellowship hall to turn it into the coffee house, art gallery, and music venue that is filled with local university students through the week," Dan adds.

Dan is very enthusiastic about this model for others because about sixty from the Presbyterian church joined about three hundred from Vintage Faith in 2008 and today attendance is about eight hundred. "Our story has been a very Kingdom-minded adventure and I think there is a lot of potential with this type of partnership," he says. "Older churches dying out that are in these wonderful, no-mortgage buildings and young church plants needing a building. And then there's the bonus of intergenerational relationships. We're breaking down barriers and embracing different viewpoints, while living out the mission of Jesus."

As you prayerfully explore ways to find potential merger partners, consider the motives that might push a church toward merging. These include the life stages mentioned in this chapter and the five major motives described in Chapter Three:

- Mission-driven mind-sets
- Economic-driven pressures
- Multisite-driven momentum
- Succession-driven strategies
- Reconciliation-driven hope
- Desire to be multiethnic

Joining Churches

Regardless if your church is strong, stable, stuck, or struggling, it may be a great candidate to join with another church locally or nationally. If your church becomes the joining church in the merger, then how would you find a suitable lead church? Look around your community. Is there a church that God is blessing and that is having a significant impact that you could join? Is there a healthy church that you have affinity with or a denominational tie that you could make to do better ministry together? Nationally, is there a church outside of your community that you align with philosophically as well as theologically? Similar thoughts could apply to churches that approach the idea as a merger of equals.

We love the question that our friend Stephen Gray asks churches that are on a declining slope in their life cycle as he helps them think through their options. He calls it his million-dollar question: "What if we were able to help you live out the vision that you were founded for in the first place, leading to an exponential impact in your community?" No church wants to close, nor does it want to live in ongoing "maintenance mode"; every church has a purpose that it wants to fill.

Your answer to these questions could be a sign that you should explore a merger from the perspective of a joining church. The Leadership Network 2011 survey of church mergers revealed that the majority of mergers are initiated by the joining church. If you believe the purpose of your church could be best fulfilled by joining another like-minded church, then don't wait to be asked; initiate the conversation.

It Takes Work to Find God's Leading

When Capstone Church of Anderson, South Carolina, was offered a five-hundred-seat sanctuary on eight acres of land in historic downtown Anderson by Central Baptist Church, it wasn't sure if it wanted to accept this gift. The offer caught Capstone Church completely by surprise.

"We had met each other just a few months before," Capstone's pastor David Barfield explained to us. "Our church had wanted to do a giveaway day to bless the community on the west side of downtown. We needed a local place to make it happen, and we had noticed Central Baptist's facility there." Each time David and the church staff drove by the church facility, they prayed about it. One day they noticed a car there, so they knocked on the church door.

Capstone was a nontraditional church of 150 people meeting in a movie theater in the suburbs. Central Baptist Church, founded in 1952, and for many years a bustling congregation of four hundred with a sanctuary that seated five hundred, now found itself located in an economically depressed, higher-crime neighborhood. It had a tall steeple, 1970s green carpet, and twelve people attending, all over age sixty. They no longer had a pastor. Though both churches were Southern Baptist, they were very different from each other in worship style and method of ministry.

The initial door-knock conversation in 2008 led to permission for a one-time Saturday use of the Central Baptist parking lot and facility. "They had a heart to touch their community but not the resources to do it," David says. "They were hesitant at first about working with us but this initial project allowed Central to begin making a difference again."

> *They had a heart to touch their community but not the resources to do it.*

After the successful event known as Give Away Day, the two churches went their separate ways. A few months later Capstone decided to do another community day. The people of Central Baptist not only said yes but also asked, "Can you help us line up a preacher for our Sunday services?"

A few months later they asked again to meet with David. "I thought they were planning to ask me for more help with pulpit supply," he said. "But there at McDonalds over a Dr. Pepper and two coffees, two members of Central Baptist asked, "What would it be like if we gave you our church?"

Capstone was an unconventional growing church with few resources, Central was a dying conventional church with a huge facility asset. Could Capstone even afford to upgrade and maintain such a gift?

"We had no intention of asking for their facility," David says. "All we wanted was to love the people of the community. We were delighted that Central Baptist loaned us a base from which to do so. But now we had to wrestle with this significant invitation of giving us their building."

And wrestle they did—both in heartfelt prayer and in much conversation—because neither option seemed to be an obvious or clear choice. According to David, "We had a lot of costs to count: if that church failed there, we might too."

In seeking wisdom within the Capstone community, some said, "I don't think this is a good idea." Others were unsure, feeling it was just "an" idea. Others were certain it was a "God" idea.

From the launch of Capstone Church in 2002, there were people praying and planting seeds financially for a location from which to operate. Not a church but a missions operation center. Always the idea was to reclaim a "dark" storefront or warehouse. The church understood that God had already prepared both a place and a people. "Where?" was still a question. And then seven years into the mission a major possibility drops into its hands. What to do?

There were lots of potential negatives such as whether Capstone would lose people in the relocation (they did), whether it would take too much money to refit the facility (it took less than expected), whether those who made the move would be willing to invite friends (they did), whether Central Baptist would dislike the changes and go back on their promises (they didn't on either count), or how to shift from occasional serve days to living in a place where need was constant (Capstone's decision was to give until they give out, whether food or clothes or light bulbs). In fact, David showed us a fourteen-item list of concerns that Capstone members had voiced, and a nine-item list that Central Baptist developed.

The church and its leaders determined to keep listening and praying. "The decision had to come from God, because no one was manipulating it," he affirms. "We knew that every location we've used as a church—a school, hotel, and movie theater—has given us opportunity to reach a different type of people. We wanted to reach out to people on the fringes in the downtown community; was this building the kind of structure and location that would help us connect with folks that have been bypassed and left behind?"

David remembers his emotions going back and forth like a pendulum. "Selfishly, I remember thinking, I do not want to pastor there," he says. "But God wants a brightly burning light right there in that area. And this is not about our opinion, but what God wants us to do."

This going back and forth went on for weeks for David, the staff, the elders, and the church. "We walked the streets, counted the cost financially, talked about whether people would drive there, and queried the church's college group and ministry groups," he says. And was it coincidence or divine leading that David had been doing a sermon series on Moses, Joshua, and the promised land when the merger opportunity arose?

Ultimately they decided that this is where God wants us. "It wasn't a lightning bolt moment, and it seemed to take forever, but it actually took only several months."

After deciding, they next had to go back to the members of the joining church and help them through the process of releasing their 45,000 square feet, $8,500 bank account, and eight acres to Capstone. Total cost to Capstone was about $200,000, mostly for renovations and also for legal fees, much of which the Capstone congregation raised in a special offering over three weeks.

The joining church clearly felt good about passing on the legacy and mission to another congregation carrying their Baptist banner but, as David confides, "I know Capstone didn't do things the way Central did on many fronts and I'm sure that was a little scary to them, but all agreed the results of touching the neighborhood for Christ were more important than traditions." After the merger, most of the joining church members soon moved on to a more traditional church. "That was a little bittersweet, but we understood," David says. "We blessed the legacy they left us, and they stayed long enough to see what God was up to. They saw that we're putting a dent in the darkness of the area we serve every week, that genuine love was being shown, and to them that was the confirmation they needed to know that the hand of God was in the merger."

After Capstone Church took formal possession of the Central Baptist facility, Capstone closed it for three months for renovations before reopening it with a new name, style, and structure. Within two years of the merger, Capstone Church had doubled in attendance to three hundred, with the average age decreasing by ten years. The last five of the original remaining attendees stayed with Capstone for nearly two years and then departed on a positive note for a more traditional-style church.

David is thrilled about the new facility and location because of what they represent. "Buildings are not sacred; it's what happens inside the building that is sacred," he says. "Church is not about where you meet; it's who you meet and who you meet with." To Capstone Church, its new location is not the promised land of comfort but a promised land as a launching point for mission.

The story is not finished. Capstone continues to partner with and serve other churches to provide leadership with worship and teaching as well as volunteers for kids and community programs. They have stated goals to reclaim kingdom property for kingdom purposes. They are working diligently to replant, reorganize, or reignite churches to become vital to the communities in which they are located.

How to Discern If Merging Is the Right Thing

The only way a merger can truly succeed is if every step is conducted with prayer, integrity, and healthy communication. There must also be a sense of discernment that this irreversible decision is consistent with God's leading.

How did Capstone determine if this merger was right for them? Pastor David Barfield was preaching through the book of Joshua when the offer came to

> *The only way a merger can truly succeed is if every step is conducted with prayer, integrity, and healthy communication.*

Capstone. Through a series of confirming scriptures, the members of the congregation believe they heard God's voice that this was their "promised land to possess." They saw God's hand through circumstances that they did not orchestrate or particularly desire. It knocked on their door. They sought God's wisdom as they counted the cost. Though the merger cost Capstone about $200,000 in legal fees and building upgrades, God provided all the money without borrowing.

David's advice to other church leaders concerning church mergers is that "if it's a God-thing, it will happen. Don't try to manipulate it or make it happen. It needs to be a natural, organic, indigenous process. Then keep your eyes peeled for potholes to step into."

So what are the steps in determining of a merger is right for your church?

Begin with Vision

Vision is the starting point of any successful merger. Does it make kingdom sense to join forces? Is it congruent with the mission and vision of both churches? Could both congregations be stronger by teaming up under one name and vision? Would their community be better served by merging? Could they accomplish more for God's kingdom together?

Initiate the Conversation

Whether your church is strong, stuck, or struggling—someone has to initiate the conversation. Lead churches may be hesitant out of courtesy or fear of their motives being misunderstood. Joining churches may be reluctant out of pride or fear of being taken over, but someone needs to start the conversation. Pray, be bold, and take the first step.

Define the Relationship

Each merger has a unique footprint. There is no one-size-fits-all formula. To use the categories we introduced in Chapter Two, some mergers are like rebirths, others like marriages, others like adoptions, and others like intensive care units. Review the circles presented in Figure 6.1 as a visual reference.

Build on Common DNA

Like any blending of families, the more that two congregations share in common, the less difficult the adjustment. The closer the DNA of two congregations, the less traumatic the transition. The less of a match, the more unpredictable the outcome. What common beliefs, values, style, and culture do the two congregations share? How much of the DNA is a match?

Integrate Unique Strengths

What does each congregation uniquely bring to the table? What are the assets to leverage—teaching, best practices, staff, money, programs, outreaches, facilities, location, reputation, history? What are the individual strengths that can complement the union? What can be affirmed from the past history? What can be celebrated and incorporated into a future together?

Identify the Differences

Building on the common DNA and unique strengths is the right foundation but ultimately the differences between the two congregations will cause the most tension and demand the greater degree of attention. Most mergers underestimate the difficulties in navigating the small degree of differences, especially cultural ones. What are the differences that could derail this merger?

Know the Financial Realities

What is the financial condition of both congregations? Are there cash-flow problems, debt, or salary incongruities? If there are facilities involved, how much will it cost to renovate and upgrade? Can the churches afford this merger? Will the return be worth the investment?

Assess All Relationships

Besides the issues already mentioned, don't forget to address denominational ties, governance, titles, staff, and ministry programs. Will you integrate, reassign, replace, redefine, eliminate— or a combination of all—when it comes to elders, deacons, staff, programs, and affiliations? Leave no stone unturned.

Establish a Timeline

When two congregations conclude that the potential benefits of merging outweigh the drawbacks of staying separate, then the merger process can begin. Most happen quickly and are done within a year; others can take longer. There are a lot of moving parts, but try to apply the basic stages outlined in Chapter Four:

- *Exploration* between the two senior leaders first, then the two senior leadership teams
- *Negotiation* of the issues between the two senior leadership teams
- *Implementation* with a public announcement to initiate the phased integration of the two congregations

- *Consolidation* as two congregations become one church
- *Integration* as the two congregations learn to live together as one church

Do a God Check

Is there a profound sense that God is in this? Is there a compelling awareness that this is something the Holy Spirit has orchestrated? Are your motives God-honoring? Has the Bible spoken to you about this merger? Have wise and objective advisors affirmed it? Is there a strong sense that "if we don't do this, we're being disobedient to the promptings of the Holy Spirit"?

Don't move forward with a merger if you don't see God's fingerprints all over it. As pastor David Barfield told us, "Go into it with your eyes looking for landmines. If you don't spot the potential pitfalls, you'll fall into them. A lot of entrepreneurs like me want to make things happen in our own strength, and it's hard to sit back to let God do it."

Take a Vote or Survey

Finally, if the leadership of both congregations concludes that God is leading them to propose a merger to their respective congregations, then the final decision is ready to be made. In most cases it is wise for both congregations to have several public meetings to explain the terms, benefits, and process of the merger and to address all their questions. Sometimes the lead church may require a vote of its congregation but the joining church should always take a vote or at least a poll because churches don't join churches; people do. A vote or poll honors the members and will help create broader ownership for the outcome.

Both church leadership teams need to decide what minimum affirmation percentage is acceptable. Should they merge if the vote is less than 90 percent, 75 percent, or 50 percent? Every church has to decide what its comfort level of acceptance is.

The Leadership Network 2011 survey of church mergers revealed that most churches do take votes (both the lead church and the joining church), and the vast majority of those votes are between 80 percent and 100 percent in favor of a merge.

Evaluating Potential Merger Partners

One of the most thorough examples we found of how one joining church initiated the merger conversation was the 109-year-old Oak Community Church in suburban Chicago. Oak Community concluded that joining a multisite church was the best option for its declining congregation of 125. It owned a debt-free campus including a 288-seat worship center, a youth house, and a parsonage, all together worth over $3 million. It also had $400,000 in the bank. Its interim pastor and leadership team created an introductory letter to initiate the merger conversation, which they sent to several multisite churches in their area.

They developed a list of questions in the following ten categories for each candidate church to address in writing before they would meet with them:

- *Transition process:* How would the merger occur and how long will it take?
- *Philosophy of ministry:* How similar are our styles of ministry?
- *Staff:* How would you staff postmerger and what would happen to our current staff?
- *Organization:* How would the staff and ministries be organized? Who would report to whom?
- *Finances:* What happens to the money given at our location and who determines the budget?
- *Missionaries:* What happens to the missionaries who are dependent on our financial support?
- *Ministries:* What will happen to our current ministries?

- *Facilities:* What are your long-term goals for our facilities?
- *Doctrinal:* How similar are we doctrinally?
- *Other:* Anything else we need to know about?

Then they evaluated the different multisite churches they might join, grading each candidate church on an academic scale of A to F based on the response to the ten questions, combined with their own onsite observations:

- *Teaching:* How will the teaching be delivered (in person or videocast)?
- *Worship:* Will the worship style be contemporary or traditional?
- *Programs:* What programs will be integrated, recalibrated, or eliminated?
- *Flexibility:* How accommodating will you be with our way of doing ministry?
- *Team approach:* How much input will we have in the way our ministry is done postmerger?
- *Timing:* How quickly could you begin the merger process?
- *Name recognition:* How well known is your church in our community?
- *Experience:* How capable are you in successfully navigating a church merger?
- *Proximity:* How close is your church to our church?
- *Seeding:* How many people could your church infuse into our location?

Systematic God Checks

What about churches that have done more than one merger? As Chapter One explained in the examples of LifeChurch.tv, North Point, Eagle Brook, and others, a rising number of larger churches experience success with one, two, or three mergers and then move to develop tools so they can more systematically assess the viability for possible mergers with other churches.

For example, Ginghamsburg Church, a United Methodist congregation just north of Dayton, Ohio, has created a detailed feasibility study template to guide Ginghamsburg's leadership as they prayerfully consider whether a particular merger makes sense for their situation. The idea, according to Karen Smith, operations director, is not to replace the role of prayer but to provide helpful guidelines. "A feasibility study won't make the decision for you," she says, "but it can reveal if there are significant barriers that could prevent a merger from being successful, since these evaluations are both an art and a science."

Ginghamsburg's most recent merger is with the hundred-plus-year-old Fort McKinley United Methodist Church, which in 2008 was a fading congregation of only forty weekly attendees in an economically challenged neighborhood about fifteen miles from Ginghamsburg. Today it's a vibrant church of over four hundred attendees and is bringing new life and hope to its at-risk community and changing the world one life at a time—locally, nationally, and globally. This includes a weekly Sunday breakfast that serves about four hundred, Tuesday night dinner that serves over 130 with related Bible study that draws almost fifty, a food pantry and clothing shop that serves three to four hundred families per month, a GED program with twenty to twenty-five students, Project Neighborhood that has touched 181 different households, and classes in life skills, parenting, financial counseling, and marriage. The weekly offerings tripled between premerger in 2008 and postmerger in 2011. This merged church has skin in the game.

Most people at the church describe the process as a restart. Marilyn Hess, a member there for more than sixty years, grew up in the church and now serves in the church's food pantry and on its board. "Tears come to my eyes many Sundays," she says. "I never thought I'd see another era of great activity, enthusiasm, and service in this church."

Marilyn and her husband, Hugh, were part of the prayer meetings and vote to join with Ginghamsburg. They had to process some tough questions such as whether they'd be willing to give up their traditional choir and singing from hymnals. "I remember asking, 'How many of our traditions do we have to get rid of?'" says Marilyn, only to hear, "Any that keep people from coming to Jesus." When the issue was put that way, she was willing. "This was a dying church and we felt this neighborhood needed a church here." She voted yes.

Her husband Hugh likewise saw God's hand in the merger idea. "I didn't think the changes would be quite like this," he said shortly after the decision time. "But I voted 'yes' and stayed because it's not about me." He too saw the mission as more important than his own comfort.

Although it's important for the people of the joining church to sense God's leading, there is also merit in the research necessary to compile a ten- to twenty-page feasibility study. The intent, according to Karen Smith, "is to evaluate opportunity and barriers in four different areas before making a decision."

The market and culture summary compiles a side-by-side comparison of the lead church (Ginghamsburg) and the joining church (in this case Fort McKinley). "It asks who we have the potential for reaching in the target community, what is the current culture or missional DNA of the church to be acquired as well as the makeup of its congregation, and how well do the makeup and opportunities of the target community and church match up with Ginghamsburg's missional calling," says Karen. It starts with each church's mission statement and related branding and suggests the cultural impact of the merger. Areas examined include ministry organizational structure, worship style, attendance and growth patterns, and target audience. It also looks at demographics of each church, such as using census data from a combination of ZIP codes for population, median age, race, median household income, and percentage of individuals below the poverty level.

The operational and technical summary takes a hard look at the joining church's facilities and existing ministries. It itemizes the worship, media, and sound equipment and the condition of each major item. Same with office equipment. The physical plant profile looks at square footage room by room, seating, parking size and condition, plus HVAC (heating, ventilation, and air conditioning). Detailed notes describe disadvantages, such as the condition of the bathrooms, issues with handicap access, roof condition, and adequacy of existing lighting. Ginghamsburg funded an environmental study that examined for asbestos, mold, water intrusion, and lead paint. Another table summarized personnel and ministries. It covered budget issues related to finding and installing a campus pastor, makeup and function of the board, and an overview of all church ministry—both current status and current options in a merger. This section amounted to several pages covering everything from children's ministry to the church's community food pantry. Its details described, for example, the existing GED-completion program and outlined how it could be merged with the appropriate department at Ginghamsburg. It also detailed who is paid, how much, and what they do, in this case a pastor, janitor, secretary, choir director, organist, bell choir director, senior citizen's director, and childcare providers—most on a very part-time basis.

The section on financial due diligence covers a wide range of issues. The ideal, according to Karen, is "a church with no debt and that still has funds available to address immediate issues identified by the study should a merger move forward." Areas include current giving patterns, current operational costs, review of any indebtedness and financial assets, insurances, tax status documentation, and claims and litigation records, if any. The point of the study is to outline existing issues and a potential process for moving forward. For example, bank accounts would be opened and managed by the Ginghamsburg CFO. All current Fort McKinley monies and investments would be moved into these new accounts. All Fort McKinley ministries post-merger would be subject to the same financial controls that exist currently at Ginghamsburg. Future projects are also itemized, from installation of a monitored fire detection system to wireless microphones, with timing tiers also noted (one, two, or three, depending on immediacy).

The final section includes study recommendations and next steps. It advises whether the merger should move forward and if so what the next steps might be. Once the decision to merge was made, a more detailed document with about fifty action steps was created, each line noting a projected start and finish date and who would be responsible for making it happen.

Even with all this due diligence, Ginghamsburg leaders always return to the issue of changed lives. As Karen says, "The greatest confirmation was the signs of transformation in the surrounding community—new neighborliness and hope, new community partnerships achieving results together, and people within the neighborhood who started calling 'the Fort' their church even though they may never have set foot in the door."

The feasibility study took many hours, the talents of many people, and a few costs, such as the environmental test. Ginghamsburg has already used the feasibility study document in evaluating other potential mergers, recommending one church for an ongoing mentoring relationship with Ginghamsburg and rejecting another. "The match with our calling is of first importance," says Karen. "For instance, we didn't move forward with one church because the community was at a higher socioeconomic level than we felt called to reach. Second, it had a great opportunity with college students at a university literally across the street. We do college ministry but it is not an area in which we have a strong, proven track record of success. One again, not a match."

But yet they keep looking. As campus pastor Dave Hood says, "How many near-empty buildings are awaiting a mighty work to be done in them?"

10

HOW TO START THE MERGER CONVERSATION

Healthy mergers usually are the result of a relationship built on mutual respect and trust. As you build relationships with local pastors and other ministry partners to serve your community together, merger possibilities emerge.

How to approach another church about a merger seems like the million-dollar question that everyone wants to know. More often, the potential joining church initiates the conversation, but not always. As one pastor told us, "There are perhaps dozens of churches within twenty minutes of our church building. They might misunderstand us and think that all we want are their assets. The truth is that I want to help them turn the corner by joining with us and at the same time fulfill the mission of both of our churches. So I'm beginning to reach out to them."

The Leadership Network 2011 survey of church mergers asked churches how they framed the conversation and invitation to merge. Their responses fell into several categories. Here are the ones that have the broadest replicability.

Lead Church Initiates a Relationship-Based Exploratory Conversation

Several stories in this book describe a relational connection between two churches. In some the pastors knew each other, in others people in one church knew someone in the other church and introduced the appropriate leaders to each other. Most of the conversations begin with a sense of tentativeness:

- "Would you church ever consider . . . ?"
- "Is there a way we could partner together that might be a win for both churches?"
- "I wanted to tell you that we are looking toward launching a multisite campus in your community. Would you be interested in joining with us?"

We're very impressed with Scott Chapman, a senior pastor at The Chapel in greater Chicago (mentioned in Chapter One). His church is multisite and several of its campuses have come by mergers. He has instructed each of his campus pastors, "Find ten pastors in your zip code whom you can bless and help to thrive." With an attitude and heart like that, it's little surprise that more merger opportunities have come their way.

Lead Church Invites Potential Joining Church Pastor to Join Its Staff—and Bring His Church Along

Pastor Brandon Park initiated a merger discussion through a conversation with Bobby Gonzalez, senior pastor of another church that resulted in a rebirth merger. "We were looking for someone to oversee our outreach and church growth ministries and I asked Bobby if he would ever give consideration to coming on board with me and my staff team to serve in this capacity," Brandon explains. Bobby said that he would certainly be interested. Then, according to Brandon, "Honestly the next question in my mind was, 'How am I going to afford to pay for his salary?'" That thought led to the next idea. "Bobby, do you think your entire church would be interested in merging and becoming a part of Wayside Baptist Church of Miami?" Bobby responded that he thought that would be a viable possibility.

The other church had recently dealt with a series of setbacks. A staff infidelity issue had caused many to leave. Despite many good efforts, the church could never break the one hundred attendee barrier. They were also relegated to meeting in the warehouse district of the city, which was not conducive to growth. They were already contemplating disbanding their congregation.

When this rebirth merger happened, the people came en masse to Wayside, immediately assimilated into the existing fellowship, and began serving in many capacities. Their giving more than covered the expense of Bobby's salary. Bobby now also functions as Wayside's Spanish pastor, enabling the church to start an additional morning worship service in Spanish. "Many of the members who came through the merger are helping us with various outreach ministries as well as assisting Wayside in getting our Spanish worship service off the ground," says pastor Brandon.

Lead Church Ministers to a Hurting Church and Later Asks if It Could Do More

Another example of a rebirth merger comes from Brian Walton, lead pastor at Calvary Christian Church in Winchester, Kentucky. Brian knew of a church that had closed for all practical purposes. Sunday services hadn't been held there in almost a year. A handful of people were still loosely affiliated with the building and would gather for a handful of functions each year. An eighty-four-year-old woman maintained the building— making sure the lawn was mowed, utilities paid, and so on. She said she just felt like God had told her to wait. "We spent a number of months learning her story, asking questions, and building relationships," Brian reports. After about six months, they began a weekly Bible study on Thursday nights. "No plans were discussed, no agenda, just Bible study and relationships," Brian says. After ten weeks he asked, "Would you like to explore some ways that we could go further with this?" A few months later this dying church was reborn when they launched weekend services as it merged with Calvary Christian.

The merger experience went so well that Calvary Christian began a prayerful process toward a second merger. "I've begun meeting weekly with the pastor there," he reports. "If the Lord moves and blesses, we will eventually bring up the subject. If he doesn't, we won't."

Joining Church Asks for Help and So Lead Church Suggests the Idea of a Merger

Silver Creek Fellowship (lead church) and Northside Fellowship (joining church), about fifteen miles away from each other in Silverton, Oregon, have had a long-standing friendship and have jointly sponsored several events in the past. Silver Creek Fellowship has been experiencing growth and blessing but Northside has been through some serious leadership difficulties. As a result, the church had experienced rapid decline, going from a Sunday attendance of over 150 to about 50 in six months.

"It seemed like the church might die, so I was invited by the Northside elders to come and meet with them to give them counsel and advice," pastor Rob Barnes told us. Rob felt that God wanted him to share a scripture with them that included the lines "come with us and we will do you good" and "if you go with us, it will come about that whatever good the Lord does for us, we will do for you" (Num. 10:29, 32). Rob used it to encourage them to see that they could become a part of the blessing that God was giving us. They did, and Northside Fellowship was rebirthed by merging with Silver Creek Fellowship.

Joining Church Pursues Suitors

One of the most thorough examples we found of how one joining church initiated the merger conversation was the 109-year-old

Oak Community Church in suburban Chicago as described in Chapter Nine. It was a declining congregation of 125. After a year of focused discussions about their best options for the future, Oak Community had concluded that being adopted by a multisite church was the best choice. So it created an introductory letter to initiate the merger conversation, a list of questions, and a comparison tool to evaluate the different multisite churches, which we describe further in Chapter Nine.

Look Beyond the Walls of Your Church

One percent of the Protestant churches in your community are going to close this year. Could those churches be redeemed or revitalized through a merger with your church? Approach those churches with humility and a kingdom of God mind-set about their situation and propose the possibility.

Meanwhile, serve your community together with other churches. Build bridges of trust with other local church leaders using the following ideas:

- *Connect:* Take the initiative to get acquainted. You share a common geography, why not share friendship over a cup of coffee?
- *Resource:* Share information, materials, and training freely. Make your expertise available. Develop coaching or mentoring opportunities.
- *Partnership:* Collaborate together in areas of common interest and for the common good of the community.

The community will be better served, local churches will be strengthened, and the kingdom of God will be extended. Mergers are more likely to grow out of that soil.

If you are a multisite church, merger opportunities will most likely present themselves to you. Often a local church in your community or beyond will initiate a conversation with you about a possible merger. The more clear you are on your church's mission, vision, values, and strategy the more effectively you can entertain whether a merger makes sense. Driving distance is also a factor. Most mergers in our survey occurred within a thirty-minute drive between the two congregations. The farther away from each other, the greater the community and cultural differences to overcome. Yet long-distance mergers can be successful when there is a strong identification with the mission, vision, values, and strategy of the lead church.

The church landscape across the United States is being transformed by realignments of churches around a compelling mission and often sharing a common theological orientation. These new alignments or "tribes" are coming out of a mutual desire for greater impact. They are motivated by the strength of synergistic possibilities that a merger offers, "Two are better than one . . . and a cord of three strands is not quickly broken" (Eccles. 4:9, 12). They are the new mini-denominations that are exponentially growing as a result of mergers of mutually healthy and like-minded churches. If your church has a compelling mission and strategy to reach more people and extend its influence, then invite other churches to join you who share your cause.

If you are drawn to a church out of a shared sense of mission, a common denomination, or network affiliation, initiate the conversation and get the discussion going.

However, if you are drawn to a church out of a shared sense of mission, a common denomination, or network affiliation, initiate the conversation and get the discussion going.

Pursue Reconciliation Where Needed

Is your church the cause or the result of a church split that occurred years ago? If so, most likely there is a need for a healing and reconciliation. Even if a merger isn't the outcome, reconciliation is the right thing to pursue; it is honoring God and bringing a powerful testimony to the larger community. As Jesus prayed, "May they be brought to complete unity to let the world know that you sent me . . ." (John 17:23). The Apostle Paul challenged the church at Philippi:

> If you have any encouragement from being united with Christ, if any comfort from his love, if any fellowship with the Spirit, if any tenderness and compassion, then make my joy complete by *being like-minded*, having the same love, *being one in spirit and purpose*. Do nothing out of selfish ambition or vain conceit, but in humility consider others better than yourselves. Each of you should look out not only to your own interests, but also to the interests of others (Phil. 2:1–4, emphasis added).

Someone has to take the first step toward a reconciliation. Could it be you? It could result in a reunion merger like the Louisiana churches we mentioned in Chapter Three.

Build Multiethnic Bridges

Do you desire to be a more inclusive multiethnic church? Reach out to the local minority church and partner together in serving your community. Visit the services, take the pastor to lunch, exchange pulpits, develop a friendship, and see how God leads. Finding or becoming a good merger candidate starts with being a good neighbor to other churches in your community. As you serve together the community that you share in common, you may discover a comradeship that introduces the possibility of merging together. This approach is not for the faint of heart, but it can reap exponential kingdom gain

Finding or becoming a good merger candidate starts with being a good neighbor to other churches in your community.

as you demonstrate the power of the gospel to bring diverse groups together under the banner of Jesus.

We were intrigued by a pastor who added this comment to the Leadership Network 2011 survey of church mergers: "You didn't ask why we merged." He went on to explain that he was pastoring an established church that was in transition from a traditional model of ministry to a more contemporary one. His church was also trying to transition to become a neighborhood church once again. "As the community began to change and members moved to the suburbs we found we were losing a grip on the community the church was in," he said. Part of the change was a growing Hispanic community that "we desired to reach but weren't able to do." He developed a relationship with a Hispanic pastor in the community and they partnered to reach the community.

That effort led to a formal merger of the two churches. "Now we are a multigenerational, multiethnic, and multicultural church that not only reflects the community but is also finally poised to reach the whole community," the pastor concluded.

> *Now we are a multigenerational, multiethnic, and multicultural church that not only reflects the community but is also finally poised to reach the whole community*

The Kind of Leader a Merger Needs

What kind of leader does a merger need? What are the qualities needed in a leader to successfully navigate a church merger?

The oft-quoted phrase "everything rises or falls on leadership" is certainly appropriate for church mergers. Successful church mergers do not happen without effective leadership. Even though no two church mergers are alike, there are some common qualities in the type of leader required to skillfully lead churches down the merger pathway.

All great leaders do three things. They define reality: "Where are we now?" They cast a vision for the future: "This is where we want to go!" And they chart the course: "This is the way to the future; follow me."

> *All great leaders do three things. They define reality. . . . They cast a vision for the future. . . . And they chart the course.*

Those who have successfully led churches through a merger tend to be winsome individuals who are kingdom minded, mission driven, strategic thinking, get-it-done individuals. They are able to rise above their specific circumstances and help others see the bigger picture of possibility. They are strong leaders but not overbearing. They know how to motivate people and build teams. They are bold but gracious. They exude confidence without being arrogant. They are able to keep a calm head in the midst of chaos. They are tough skinned enough to endure the criticisms, but tenderhearted enough to love the people regardless. They not only lead the people but genuinely love them through the process.

A great example is Mark Jobe, pastor of New Life Community Church in downtown Chicago. In 2008 a Lutheran church that had existed for 114 years was reborn by merging with New Life. The church had been struggling and declining since the 1990s and eventually the congregation and the sponsoring denomination agreed it was time to close the church. The touching story unfolded in this way:

> On the day of the dissolution, some two hundred people gathered for the ceremony. It was an emotional time of memories, prayers, and a final Holy Communion for Bethel Evangelical Lutheran Church.
>
> The printed program specified that at the end of the service Ralph Kirchenberg [the seventy-year-old president of the church

board] would give the keys to Mark Jobe, as lead pastor of New Life Community Church. Both stood and Ralph began to speak. "It says in the program that we are to hand over the keys to New Life at this point," he said, "but you know this is really not about keys or buildings."

At this point every eye was on this senior saint whose entire life had been spent in ministry in the closing church. "This is about something a lot more important than buildings and keys." Ralph paused to open a package he had brought with him. From it he pulled out a framed plaque. "It's become popular in recent years for organizations and companies to craft a mission statement, and Bethel has also had its own mission statement. So today we're not really giving you the keys to this building as much as the mission of Bethel Evangelical Lutheran Church."

He took the plaque, held it up, and read it aloud. The mission statement was a very straightforward, powerful expression of sharing the gospel, bringing transformation, and loving the community. It was the type of mission statement that any church which loves Jesus and wants to serve the gospel would be able to endorse. "Mark, we give our mission to New Life, to carry it forward into our community," he concluded.

There wasn't a dry eye in the place. The closing of the church was a reminder to everyone that this wasn't a death, nor was it really even a merger. It was a new means of carrying Christ's mission forward to reach a new generation.[1]

Mark Jobe exemplifies the kind of lead pastor that is most conducive to facilitating healthy church mergers. His infectious heart for God, relational skills that communicate both vision and care with well-developed team-building practices has led New Life Community Church to become a fifteen-campus church with over 4,500 attending in the heart of Chicago primarily through church mergers. May his tribe increase!

Humility Goes a Long Way

In many of our discussions with church leaders we heard a recurring emphasis on the importance of humility in church mergers. Churches that are stuck or in decline need humility to acknowledge they are struggling. It takes humility to admit my church is not doing well and needs a new start. Lead churches need to also have humility about their role in shepherding new people toward a new vision and not coming in as though they have every answer to every problem.

Mergers are built on trust and faith. Trust is earned by demonstrating genuine love and concern for the joining congregation, not just their facilities, assets, or increased attendance. Faith is extended by the joining congregation when they believe the lead church is trustworthy. Mergers have to be approached as two teams humbly uniting around the same vision. This point cannot be emphasized enough. Successful mergers are not about us, but about extending God's kingdom.

Humility goes a long way. As we overheard one pastor say as he led his congregation and a joining church through a merger, "The largest room in the world is the room for improvement."

11

SELF-ASSESSMENT FOR MERGER READINESS

It's hard to find a church that couldn't be considered as a candidate for a merger, either as a lead or joining church. We especially believe that the merger option may be the best option for many of the 80 percent of churches in the United States that are stuck or struggling. So is *your* church merger ready?

Only God knows if a merger is right for your congregation at this time, and if so, with what other church or churches. If you're reading this chapter to find out if you're ready to do a merger, we assume you've already followed the guidance of the previous two chapters by seeking God in prayer and confirmation of the Holy Spirit's leading down the merger path. Please do not bypass this vital step of affirming your heart's desire to know and follow God's will and timing. Certainly include your church board, other leaders, and as appropriate, the entire congregation in the discernment process. If you're part of a denomination, work as closely as possible with those in authority over your church who can bless or block a merger.

Key Indicators

Your self-assessment process will depend on whether you are the lead church or the joining church in the merger. If your situation is the more rare merger of two equals, then still review all of the following questions.

Remember that the average time for a merger in the Leadership Network survey was seven to ten months between the initial discussion and the merger actually happening. So when you're ready, things might move very quickly.

For each of these questions, the framing decision is whether merging is likely to lead to a better answer.

All lead and joining churches:

- To what extent are the hopes, dreams, and potentials of your church being fulfilled at present?
- Would you categorize your church as strong, stuck, struggling, or declining? How satisfied or dissatisfied are you with that status?
- Could your church mission be accomplished better in a merger relationship with another church rather than alone?
- Is there a specific church you would consider merging with?
- Has your church been approached by another church to consider merging?
- How willing is your church to take risks and be open to change?
- How strongly does your church really want to grow numerically?
- How convinced are you that a merger is likely to increase the spiritual health and growth of your membership?

If you're likely to be the lead church:

- Does your church have a clear mission, vision, and a set of stated values?
- How does a merger help fulfill your church's mission?
- Does your church have a multisite strategy?
- How open and prepared are you for the opportunity to become multisite through a merger?
- Has your church outgrown its facility?

- Is your church healthy and growing at least by 5 percent a year?
- Does your church have people living in the area of the merged church?
- Can your church give away 10 percent of its people to a church merger and still be healthy?
- Is the dream for your church bigger than its current capacity to fulfill it?
- Has your church set aside money to fund merger costs?
- Does your denomination or network have funds or assistance available for a merger?

If you're likely to be the joining church:

- Has your church been declining for more than three years? If so, how capable are you, given your present resources, to make the major changes necessary to turn your church around?
- How closely does your church reflect the composition of the surrounding community? Is the profile of your church moving toward or away from the average age, ethnicity, and education level of your church's immediate community?
- How likely is it that your church will exist ten years from now if things continue at their present rate?
- Is your church without a pastor, having difficulty finding one, or not likely to find one when your present pastor leaves?
- How strong is the financial viability of your church without outside help? Is it moving toward being financially stronger or weaker?
- Do you want your church to flourish even if it means giving its leadership and assets to another church?
- Does your congregation and leadership sense an urgency to make the major changes that a merger will represent?

Alternatives to Merging

One way to determine your church's readiness to merger is to explore alternatives. Your answers to the previous questions might not mean that a merger is your best pathway. For example, instead of merging, you might consider the following:

- Change your worship style.
- Change the pastor.
- Change other leadership.
- Change the mission.
- Change location (relocate).
- Close or dissolve.
- Continue in the current location with the same programming.
- Continue in the current location and tap into building equity to fund new programs.
- Share your campus with two or more congregations that jointly own and use one facility. This is not a landlord-tenant–shared building situation but janitorial, maintenance, and office staff are shared, the facility is owned by a nonprofit corporation that is controlled by the congregations, and a joint board coordinates the shared use of the building and allocates expenses.[1]
- Rent your church facility to other groups. The website www.rentmychurch.com offers free and paid postings to match renters with available space nationwide.
- Close the church and tap into the church's property equity to provide funds for a restart and to give the building a face-lift.
- Sell the current property and relocate the congregation.
- Sell the church's property and give funds to a church-planting organization to start one or several new churches,

or place funds in an endowment to build new churches perpetually.

- Sell the church's property and give funds to several nonprofit organizations.[2]

Comparison Profile Exercise

Jim Tomberlin encourages churches that have a potential merger partner to make a side-by-side comparison profile of the two churches. Often when the two church teams see the comparisons, the similarities and differences stand out. Here are the categories he uses, with an explanation of each:

- *Mission, vision, and values.* Reveals how close or how far the two churches are in their overall purpose and philosophy of ministry
- *Staff.* A quick snapshot of the number of paid staff at both churches
- *Budget and debt.* Reveals the financial health and challenges
- *Worship center seating.* To determine capacity and use
- *Average weekend attendance by age groups (adults, students, children).* Reflects the composition of each church
- *Average age of congregation.* Reveals who each church is serving and reaching
- *Baptisms (or similar indicator of conversion growth).* A reflection of outreach or lack of it
- *Church life stage (growing, stable, stuck, struggling, declining).* Helps each church to see its own reality
- *Assets (own or rent).* Identifying the physical assets and potential liabilities each church brings to the table
- *Travel time between churches.* Most mergers are within thirty minutes travel time of each other

- *Who initiated merger possibility?* Helps in framing the conversation between the two churches
- *What initiated merger conversation?* Reveals the possible motivations for merger possibility

Are you a candidate for a church merger? If your church has a clear mission to reach people and extend its impact locally, then your church is in a strong position to embrace another church through a merger. If your church believes it could become a better church or be turned around by joining another like-minded but more vibrant church, then it is a good candidate for a church merger.

12

EXERCISE

Identifying Your Merger Issues

As a blues musician might sing, "You've got issues, I've got issues, everyone has issues, including churches." So do churches, especially churches that are merging together. Of the churches that Jim has walked through the merger process, two churches in Arizona are the closest to a textbook case of an adoption merger that employed all the steps and tools we recommend in the book.

In fall 2010, co-lead pastors Scott Ridout and Chad Moore of Sun Valley Community Church in Gilbert, Arizona, initiated a conversation with the senior pastor of the Bethany Community Church in neighboring Tempe to let him know of their plans to start a multisite campus in his area. These pastors had served their congregations side by side in the same greater community together for two decades, although their churches were at two different stages in their life cycles. Sun Valley had been growing steadily since the church started in 1990 and was bursting at the seams with nearly four thousand in weekend services. Bethany Community Church was in a seventeen-year decline. It was down to one service with eight hundred people attending there. Meanwhile Sun Valley had hundreds of families attending from Tempe, where Bethany was located.

In that initial conversation Scott and Chad proposed the possibility that instead of starting a new campus, would Bethany consider joining forces to become one church with Sun Valley? After many conversations between these leaders, a dialogue began with the elders of Bethany and the Sun Valley leadership.

Initially, Bethany's elders made the decision not to pursue the idea of a merger. This culminated in the senior pastor, courageously and humbly, resigning. He stated his reasons for resigning was his love for the church, his inability to turn the church around, and the belief that he was not the right pastor to lead them into the future. He graciously tendered his resignation with the hope his departure would be a catalyst for the change that was needed for a better future.

Two months later the elders restarted the conversation with Sun Valley, resolved some earlier misunderstanding, and, with the prayer support of Sun Valley's leaders, began to wrestle through the best scenario for the future of Bethany. After numerous meetings, discussions, and lots of prayer seeking God's will, both leadership teams agreed to hire Jim Tomberlin to assist them in exploring the feasibility and desirability of the two churches becoming one through what can best be described as an adoption process.

Both churches moved through the various merger stages and within ten months of the initial conversation with the senior pastor, the Bethany elders recommended to their congregation "to join forces with Sun Valley Community Church," posting the explanation on the Bethany church website.

The recommendation required a 75 percent approval by the membership. It passed by 80 percent and became Sun Valley Community Church–Bethany Campus three months later.

Identifying Their Issues

At one point in this story the Bethany elders voted by an overwhelming majority to recommend the merger. How exactly did they get to that point? How did they determine the bridges that needed to be crossed for a merger to happen?

Every church, after determining through prayer and thoughtful dialogue that a merger is possible, will need to create a feasibility report that summarizes any number of issues, especially the

Merger Recommendation

On Sunday, July 17, the Elder Board announced to the congregation their recommendation that Bethany Community Church join with Sun Valley Community Church to become one church on multiple campuses. Our two churches have very similar statements of faith, visions, and missions. We have a long history of working together programmatically and in the community. This decision came after several months of exploration, discussion, and, most importantly, prayer that God reveal His plan for Bethany. The Elders believe that this is God's will for the next chapter in the life of Bethany Community Church.

This recommendation did not come lightly and we know that you will have many questions as to why and how this will work. The membership vote on this recommendation is set for the last Sunday in September. Between now and then there will be many opportunities for the Elders to provide more detailed information on the recommended merger, and for you to ask questions, give input, dialogue, and pray. In the meantime you can contact the elders by e-mail, in the Worship Center on Sunday mornings, or by phone. We ask that each of you take this time to actively and earnestly seek God's will for the future of Bethany Community Church.

Over the next few months, we will use this page to record additional information, timelines, meeting notices, and other important information as they are announced.

Other helpful documents:

- Register for Elder Home Meetings
- Adoption Recommendation Timeline
- Change Is Coming to Bethany
- Bethany FAQs
- Sun Valley Community Church Constitution and Bylaws
- Merger Recommendation Announcement

problematic ones that need to be resolved if a merger is going to happen. It should cover the following questions:

- Are we compatible in fundamental doctrine and practice?
- Are we similar enough to merge?

- What are the issues that need to be addressed?
- What are the issues that would prevent a merger from occurring?

Every church merger is different and has a unique "church print." There is no one-size-fits-all formula to follow, but all will have to address the same issues. Which issues are the most important and how and when they will be addressed vary from church to church, but all issues have to be addressed, and it's better to do so sooner rather than later.

Following are twenty-five issues that should be addressed in every church merger. It is recommended that the leadership teams of each church review these twenty-five issues separately and identify the problematic ones. Then review each other's list together. Perhaps most of the items will be nonissues but they still need to be addressed.

Usually three to five problematic issues surface that could be deal breakers. The most common problematic issues revolve around the pastor and staff, worship styles, the role of women in the church, how to handle debt or financial matters, the level of denominational engagement, and the transfer of assets. If the two leadership teams can find a resolution to these problematic issues, then a merger is feasible and can be recommended to their churches for a vote. The time between the recommendation to merge and the vote is when the two congregations are determining if this merger is desirable. This process will also give both churches the information needed for a set of public FAQs (frequently asked questions) as they present the merger to their respective congregations.

Specific Issues to Address

Here is an annotated list of the twenty-five issues every church merger has to address. You can see in Appendix B how Sun Valley Community Church and Bethany Community Church specifically addressed every issue. It is very thorough and a good template for other church leaders to review as they work through their merger deliberations.

Doctrine

- *Theological beliefs.* How do the two churches compare theologically? Are their heritages charismatic, reformed, or dispensational? Do they share similar or divergent views on the Bible, baptism, spiritual gifts, divorce, and the role of women?
- *Governance.* How similar or different are the two churches when it comes to local church government? Are they congregational or episcopal? Is each church elder governed or staff led?
- *Affiliations.* Are the two congregations' members of the same denomination, network, or association? If not, is there compatibility? Are the affiliations mandatory? Will they remain or change?

Philosophy of ministry

- *Mission.* How does each church answer the question, "Why do we exist?" An honest answer will reveal how close or far apart they are on the primary purpose of the church. The strongest mergers are those that are primarily mission driven.

  The strongest mergers are those that are primarily mission driven.

- *Vision.* Vision is a picture of your preferred future. How does each church answer the question, "If we succeed in fulfilling our mission as a church, what would our church look like ten years from now?" How similar are the two visions? Are the two congregations creating a new vision together? If not, can each embrace the vision of the other church?

- *Values*. Values are the principles that guide how a church does its ministry. They reflect what really matters to a church. How similar or divergent are your values?

- *Strategy*. Effective churches develop strategies to implement their mission and fulfill their vision. Are you drawn to or repelled by the way the other church does ministry?

- *Worship style*. How similar or different are the worship styles of your church from the other church? Are you contemporary, traditional, blended, or something else? Is your worship style more participatory or performance oriented? Does your church have choirs or worship bands, drums or organs, pews or theater seats, stained glass or video screens? Often worship style is a primary basis for why people like or dislike a church. If the two churches are not similar, is one willing to embrace the other's different worship style?

- *Preaching*. Who will be bringing the weekend messages to the congregation? How long is the typical message in each church? Will the sermons be delivered in person, by video, or through a combination of both?

- *Membership*. What are the requirements for church membership at your church? Will those requirements transfer to the other church? If a merger does occur, will the membership transfer automatically or will a membership class be required?

- *Programs*. What church programs and ministries are non-negotiable and therefore untouchable? What programs could be integrated into the new entity and which ones would need to be recalibrated or eliminated?

- *Budget*. Budgets reflect the priorities of a church. What do you learn about each other by reviewing their budget? What percentage goes to staff, debt reduction, ministries, and missions?

Personnel

- *Expectations*. How does each congregation understand the merger relationship? Is this merger a rebirth, an adoption, a marriage, or an ICU situation? How each party sees the merger determines its expectations of the relationship.

  > *The sooner both parties can define the relationship and get on the same page concerning expectations, the smoother the merger process will go.*

  The sooner both parties can define the relationship and get on the same page concerning expectations, the smoother the merger process will go.
- *Senior pastors*. The first question that has to be addressed if there are two senior pastors involved is the postmerger status of the senior pastor of the joining church. Will that person remain as pastor of that location if it becomes a two-campus merger, be redeployed to another staff position within the church, or be given a severance package? This issue is usually already decided between the two senior pastors in the exploration stage.
- *Staff*. Are the job descriptions, pay levels, contracts, and benefits comparable or dramatically different? What will be the staff needs in the new church entity? What staff will remain in their current position, be redeployed to another area in the church, downsized, or released? What are the severance policies?
- *Boards and committees*. Will the existing boards and committees be integrated, recalibrated, or eliminated? Will the board members stay the same? Will all, some, or none remain?
- *Missionaries*. Will funding support for the missionaries, parachurch ministries, and other organizations supported by the church be continued, phased out over time, or ended on completion of the merger?

Legal

- *Attorney.* Do you have competent legal counsel to guide you through the legal steps of a church merger? (See Chapter Seven, "Financial and Legal Costs of a Merger.")

- *Church name.* Will there be a name change for one or both congregations? How will that be decided?

- *Voting.* How will the decision to merge be decided and by whom? What does each church's bylaws require? Will a congregational vote be required? If so, what will be the process and what percentage is required for approval? Even if not required, will a vote or poll be conducted as a way for the congregation to affirm their views? What is the lowest approval percentage the two churches are willing to accept?

- *Dissolution.* What will be the dissolution process of the joining church? Will this be a strict merger, asset purchase by the lead church, or a donation by the joining church (see Chapter Seven)? What do the laws of your state or province dictate?

- *Property or facility.* What will the new church entity do with any property and facilities gained in the merger? Will the property and facilities be kept or sold? What are the legal requirements and state laws for transfer of church property? What legal counsel does each church need?

- *Assets and liabilities.* What tangible assets do the two churches bring to the table in terms of property, facilities, and equipment? Is there a written inventory of all property and equipment? Due diligence is a must to determine what repairs, maintenance costs, and hidden liabilities come with these items.

- *Debt management.* What debt does either church bring to the merger? How manageable is it?

- *Timeline.* When is the earliest possible date a merger could occur between the two churches? What are the things that need to happen and by when for a merger to occur?

Working through the issues is the hard work of merger deliberations. It is an essential step in helping both churches learn
each other's culture, identity, and other relevant issues. Every
church, like every human being, has a story. The better you know
each other going into the merger, the better the chances of the
merger being approved and the better the integration will be
postmerger. We hope this process will surface all the hidden liabilities and potential landmines that could blow up the merger.
It is a proactive step that not only helps to determine feasibility
but will also help preempt surprises and generate congregational
confidence as you demonstrate that you have done your due
diligence.

13

MANAGING PAIN AND CHANGE

It will be a new, different church. Might as well
acknowledge it and deal with it.

That write-in comment from the Leadership Network 2011 survey of church mergers says it all: Change is coming. Deal with it.

Most will agree with the quotation, imagining it through the backdrop of many different emotions—fear, loss, anger, disappointment, disillusionment, grief, uncertainty, and anticipation. The challenge is how to merge in the most God-honoring, compassionate, clear, and missionally focused way. And we hope without any unnecessary pain!

Church mergers are not for the faint of heart. In spite of all the guidelines and best practices presented in this book, church mergers are usually messy, unpredictable, and full of surprises. The positives for successful church mergers is huge but they do not come without grief, and loss. For those dedicated church elders or board members who have the awesome responsibility of overseeing their church, one day you will stand before the real head of the church and give an account of your stewardship as church leaders. On that day God's opinion is the only one that really matters. It won't be about worship preferences, denomination affiliations, skill in defining theological nuances, organizational charting of staff positions, or facility ownership. The most important question will be, "Did we make the best decisions for the sake of God's church and the furtherance of his kingdom?"

The decisions at stake are not just outward ones but also inward ones about attitude through the painful adjustments. We admire the Phoenix area pastor whose congregation became the joining church. He initiated the merger because he realized that in many ways his church was duplicating efforts of another in the same community. He then shifted to an executive pastor role in the merged congregation. He stayed two and a half years to cement the marriage between his former congregation and the comparable-size church they joined. "The merger was an attack on my own security from every angle," he said, referring to his sense of self-image and personal insecurities. "If I didn't deal with it early on, the merger wouldn't work. Even if I said the right things, people would pick up my attitude and try to put a wedge between me and the other pastor." This pastor realized that the way to walk his own congregation through the pain of merging began with himself—his attitude and heart.

Mergers are a viable option for church expansion and kingdom gain. People will leave along the way, and that's understandable. The real test of a successful merger is not that everyone remains but whether pastors and other leaders engaged their congregations at heart levels and provided genuine spiritual leadership through the merger that resulted in deeper faith and a stronger community of believers.

Insider's Look at the Process

At one of the gatherings of the elders and senior staff of Sun Valley Community Church and Bethany Community Church the group did a table exercise that captured the benefits and also the challenges of their church merger. They set four tables, each with six people. Each table was an even mix of people from both churches. Each individual was asked to anonymously identify on a 3×5 card one positive that most excited them about this merger. On a separate card, they were asked to identify their biggest concern about this merger. Then each table group summarized and shared their list. Here is a summary of what they captured:

The positives

- The greater kingdom impact of joining together
- The synergy of a united vision and strategy that propels forward momentum
- The outreach potential of reaching both younger and older generations in our city
- Maximizing our facilities

The concerns

- Dealing with change of culture, identity, and control
- Dealing with potential loss of staff, ministries, members, and friends
- Communicating vision and implementing transition in a unified, honoring, caring, and healthy way

Then each table brainstormed and presented to the whole group how they would address their concerns. They voiced a lot of helpful suggestions. They boiled them down into one single summary statement to guide the merger process forward in a healthy way: "Cast a compelling vision clearly, consistently, and repetitively with grace, mercy, and humility to both the mind and the heart." As one of the Sun Valley elders put it, "I believe it is *far more important* that Chad and Scott cast a compelling vision that helps begin to form that bond of trust between pastors and congregants. They must strike a tone of empathy for their grieving, a sense of urgency for the lost, God's unstoppable vision for their future, and lastly the compelling vision for that particular campus. I believe it's in those last few weeks of vision casting that trust is gained and faith is required."

This is great advice for every merger! But even while going forward, be prepared for the church family of the joining church to respond to a merger announcement with a whole range of emotions. The church they have loved and served is coming

to an end. Most will go through the standard human grieving stages as they get used to the idea of merging with another
church:

> *Denial:* "I can't believe this is happening to my church. I did
> not know our church was struggling, in trouble, or con-
> cerned about its future."
>
> *Bargaining:* "Can't we fix our church ourselves? Reorganize,
> relocate, reduce budget, staff, and so on?"
>
> *Anger:* "I feel kicked in the gut. I am devastated and feel
> betrayed. I liked my church the way it is and now it will
> become something I don't know or like. I gave a lot of my
> time and money to this church and now I feel like it has
> been taken away from me."
>
> *Depression:* "I am sad. I am losing the church I love. It feels
> like a death has occurred."
>
> *Acceptance:* "I will embrace the new reality, follow the lead-
> ership's decision, and trust God for the outcome. I can see
> the benefits of merging. I am excited about the next chap-
> ter of my church."

Some will get through it quickly; others will take some time.
Most will land in a good place, give the merger a try, and a few
will move on. In a typical merger that's handled well, expect to
lose up to 20 percent of the church family in the twelve months
after the merger. Seasoned church consultant Tom Bandy, introduced in Chapters Four and Six, told us, "It's my experience
that missional mergers depend on awaken-
ing the experience of Christ in the hearts

In a typical merger that's handled well, expect to lose up to 20 percent of the church family in the twelve months after the merger.

of at least 20 percent of the members of each church. That

20 percent will have the credibility to lead another 60 percent into the merger. The remaining 20 percent can and should be left behind if necessary, regardless of how much they give."

How to Change Church Culture

How do you move a church from a *can't-do* to a *can-do* culture, from an *inward* to an *outward* focus, and from a *surviving* to a *thriving* mentality? The same way all effective church leaders lead their churches. With the Bible as their foundation, they define reality, cast a vision, make tough decisions, express great faith in God, celebrate the wins, and lovingly lead with optimism and integrity. They carefully, intentionally, and prayerfully bring about culture shift.

John Kotter at Harvard Business School has done the best work on the science of change, which can help us better understand the process of shifting church culture. His book, *Leading Change*,[1] is the standard on how to drive major change though an organization. Here is his eight-step process, with our comments on how to implement them in a church merger context:

- *Establish a sense of urgency.* Effective church leaders help people see the realities around them and the opportunities before them.

- *Create the guiding coalition.* Successful church mergers gather the right mix of people from both congregations to work together in guiding the congregations to a greater future together.

- *Develop a vision and strategy.* "Without a vision the people perish," according to Solomon's reminder in Proverbs 29:8. Develop a vision that honors the past but looks to the future. When people can see a hopeful picture of the future and how to get there, many will rise to the occasion and help bring it to pass. Present the new strategy as an extension of the past that reflects the values of the joining church.

- *Communicate the change vision.* When there is a lack of communication, people will fill in the vacuum with incorrect and negative conclusions. It is vitally important to overcommunicate the reason, benefits, and process of the church merger to both congregations. Vision "leaks" and therefore needs to be repeated constantly and consistently through all the vehicles of mass communication and social media.

- *Empower broad-based action.* Move forward by involving progressive thinkers from both congregations to resolve all potential obstacles and give them permission to problem solve outside the box.

- *Generate short-term wins.* Nothing succeeds like success. Go for the early and easy wins to build credibility. Recognize, reward, and celebrate the people who make the wins possible.

- *Consolidate the gains and produce more change.* Build on the early successes to change all systems, structures, and policies that don't fit together and fulfill the vision.

- *Anchor new approaches in the culture.* Create a culture of positive success by demonstrating the impact of greater outreach, transformed lives, community impact, and kingdom gain.

We asked our friend Sam Chand, author of the very insightful book, *Cracking Your Church's Culture Code: Seven Keys to Unleashing Vision and Inspiration,*[2] for his thoughts on bringing culture change to merger situations. He told us:

> Meshing church cultures is a long process. Think of it as a marriage of two full-grown adults—let's say both parties are 45-plus years old. In getting married, they are converging their histories, habits, and cultures into one home. Their new household will go through major adjustments. An outside "counselor" (both pre *and* post), someone both credible and trusted, can be a big help.

So is honesty in love. This translates into the leaders (boards, elders, trustees, pastors, etc.) spending extended times together having tough conversations in a transparent atmosphere.

Learning from the Pain

Justin Anderson, introduced in the opening chapter as experiencing a merger of three congregations into one, blogged a year after his merger experience. He identified five critical lessons he learned. We present them here in excerpted form to demonstrate some of the pain he and his church experienced and to show how he managed it.

Lessons from the Merger

The mergers were easily the biggest thing we'd ever done, and we struggled to find people to guide us through the process. All three churches were healthy, growing, vibrant congregations. None of us "needed" each other, and none of our churches were in a position of strength or weakness as we attempted to navigate the process.

What I Learned

1. How much and how well are you really leading your church?

Theoretically, I've believed in the plurality of eldership. Prior to the merger, Praxis Church had seven elders, and I, as lead pastor, was first among equals. When we merged the churches, I became one member of a five-man leadership team charged with leading the vision and future of Redemption Church. I went from having more pastoral experience than my entire eldership combined to having the second least amount of experience.

Immediately, I realized that I hadn't really led my elders. Instead, I'd been a (mostly) benevolent dictator who was rarely questioned. I've grown more as a leader in the last five months than perhaps the previous six years combined. I'm learning more about leadership every day and see this merger as a great opportunity to gain invaluable leadership lessons.

2. Patience actually is a virtue.

At Praxis, because of our structure, youth, and culture, we made decisions very quickly and implemented them just as fast. Because of this, we often made missteps that had to be corrected, and we missed opportunities because we didn't wait to make sure our direction was the right one.

In a larger structure like Redemption Church, we've lost our ability to act as quickly as before and the wisdom of our new leadership team has served to slow our decision-making process significantly. It frustrated me at first, but I quickly saw the benefit as we reversed course on several ideas that I initially thought were best but turned out not to be. This saved us a lot of work and hardship.

3. Don't underestimate your congregation's capacity for change and vision.

Big changes, like a merger, aren't always popular. People simply don't like change, and I knew some people wouldn't like this change in particular. After finalizing plans for the merger, I expected a 5 percent rate of attrition in leadership, attendance, and money. I couldn't have been more wrong.

In the five months following our announcement, we've lost virtually nothing. No leaders left, nearly every member is still around, attendance is at record highs, and people are giving sacrificially. I significantly underestimated our people's appetite for vision, but I won't do it again.

4. Together is better—and it's the future.

Throughout the merger planning, we continually asked this core question: "Are we better together than we are apart?" Our churches were closely aligned doctrinally and philosophically, and we'd already partnered together on two significant endeavors. We often returned to the questions: Did we really need to merge? Couldn't we just continue to work closely together?

Five months into the merger, and looking forward to the exciting plans and vision on our near horizon, I firmly believe what I suspected all along—we are better together than we were apart. When it comes to vision, ideas, leadership, resources, and prayer, 1 + 1 + 1 = 10.

5. Relational connectivity is key.

In Larry Osborne's book *Unity Factor*,[3] he talks about having a three-fold unity on your leadership team: doctrinal, philosophical, and relational. I've learned a ton from Larry over the last couple years, but nothing has served us as well as his lesson on three-fold unity. We knew going into our merger discussions that we had doctrinal and philosophical unity, but the relational unity was something of a question mark.

I can't overstate how important relational unity is when you are considering a merger. Things will get tough, some conversations will be hard, and if you don't have the kind of relationships that allow honest, frank dialogue without your feelings getting hurt, it won't work.[4]

In my (Jim's) merger consulting with these churches, I found that Justin had the right balance of being a strong leader and teacher with genuine humility. There had been a long mentoring relationship with the lead church pastor for years before the idea of merging even surfaced between them. Their respectful relationship laid a solid foundation for their successful mission-driven merger.

Putting Your Feet to Faith

Like all living things, churches have a life cycle. In their early years, they grow a lot, just like a human being. As the decades go by, they often face a growing number of challenges, just as people do with their own health. But unlike humans, whose physical bodies eventually die, never making it past 120 years at most in this era, churches can begin a new life cycle. They have the potential to thrive for hundreds of years. A new life cycle can begin with a new pastor. Sometimes that new season of life comes through a merger.

Many come through the merger affirming that indeed the pain was well worth the change.

Choosing to merge for what we describe as missional motives is always better than having to merge as a last-ditch survival effort. Many come through the merger affirming that indeed the pain was well worth the change.

14

WHERE DO YOU GO FROM HERE?

Living Word Church in Pelham, Alabama, probably represents a lot of churches. A good man started it, reached people through it, ministered sacrificially, and along the way led them to acquire land and build facilities including a 280-seat auditorium. He served as the church's only pastor for twenty-five years and abruptly died of a heart attack—without a succession plan. That left his widow and about forty members with some tough decisions.

The story shifts from common to uncommon at this point. Before his death, the pastor—who had envisioned a growing church—had talked with his wife about forming a partnership with Church of the Highlands, a fast-growing Birmingham church based about twenty miles away that had begun expanding into campuses around Birmingham. The widow called Highlands on behalf of her church, saying to pastor Chris Hodges, "You can have everything if you don't sell it."

After the merger, Church of the Highlands took six weeks to renovate the building, expand parking, and add technology for its heavy emphasis on video teaching feeds. Highlands then sent a worship team to lead weekly services. Members who lived in the area were encouraged to attend that campus. Four years later, "it's our most successful campus," Chris says, "and we're in the process of enlarging the facility. One of the joining church's members told us that what has happened has been a fulfillment of their prayers for many years. That kind of story needs to happen more often!"

And the story doesn't end there. The campus also hosts a Hispanic service, which now draws more then three hundred people weekly. It had been a small church meeting in a Pelham basement and was invited to join the new Highlands campus there. "We have the same vision, the same theology," Layne Schranz, associate pastor at Highlands, said. "We realized we could do more together."[1]

More Churches Through Merging?

At the end of the day, we need more churches not fewer—but those churches need to be prevailing, life-giving, high-impact, reproducing churches, churches that are making a difference, not just taking up space or holding on. Healthy churches, like all living things, reproduce. But if a church cannot turn itself around, then is it more of a liability than an asset? Is it really wise to keep it going if it's unhealthy and irrelevant? Could not two strong churches have an even greater impact

> Our hope is that this book will stimulate further movement on revitalizing and synergizing existing churches through mergers that will result in propagating healthier, reproducing churches.

by joining forces, and ultimately through their synergy, create even more reproducing churches. Our hope is that this book will stimulate further movement on revitalizing and synergizing existing churches through mergers that will result in propagating healthier, reproducing churches.

Church mergers will be on the front burner—for many *the* next big thing—but in some ways they'll affect everyone in places where churches have been established for two or more generations. The research documents ongoing growth in this rising phenomenon, and we've tried to offer helpful language and categories to facilitate this conversation. We have drawn from surveys of hundreds of churches and personally interviewed dozens of them to bring to the surface the important trends and proven best practices. Most important, we want to write a book that would help church leaders discern if a merger is a possibility in their future, and if so, how to do it successfully.

Are you sensing the "urge to merge"? If you have become convinced that a merger could be a viable option for your church, what is your next step? Where do you go from here? Here are some suggested next steps to get you started down the road toward a church merger:

- *Define reality.* The first task of leaders is to define reality. Where is your church in its life cycle? Is it growing, plateaued, or declining? Courageous church leaders do not live in denial but embrace reality and help others to see it.

- *Clarify* the purpose of your church. What are the mission, vision, values, and strategy of your church? The more clarity you have around what God is calling your church to *be* and then *do*, the better you will be able to determine whether a merger is in the best interest of your church. If you need further help in this area, here are three must-read books: *Church Unique,*[2] *Simple Church,*[3] and *The Multi-Site Church Revolution.*[4]

- *Assess the health of your church.* Is your church a candidate to be a lead church or joining church in a merger? Is your church strong, stable, stuck, or struggling? Take the self-assessment test in Chapter Eleven to determine merger readiness and identify the merger model in Chapter Two that best describes your merger potential.

- *Do a demographic survey of your region.* What is the socioeconomic and racial makeup of the larger community you serve? Does your church attendance reflect the demographics of the larger community? What is the best way to reach and serve those beyond the walls of your church? Check out the US Census Bureau online,[5] Wikipedia,[6] and the Chamber of Commerce[7] info for your city to better understand the community you are called to reach and serve. For a thorough, scientific demographic analysis of your community, commission a Percept study for your region.[8]

- *Assess the redemptive potential of your community.* How many people are unchurched, dechurched, or antichurched in your community? There is a simple way to get a rough estimate of the outreach potential within your church's reach by simply identifying the total number of churches in your community and multiplying it by seventy-five people (the average size church in the United States), and then comparing it against the total local population figure. That will give you a rough estimate of the redemptive potential and underserved people in your community. National studies indicate that more than 80 percent of Americans do not attend church on a weekly or near-weekly basis.

- *Assess the church landscape in your community.* One percent of the churches in your community are likely to close in the next twelve months. Are any of those good candidates to merge with you? Are there any vibrant churches you may want to merge with? Are there any churches in your denomination, network, or region with whom you could initiate a merger possibility conversation? Are you engaged with any local churches in strategic ministry partnerships that could develop into a merger conversation?

- *Study this book.* Go through *Better Together: Making Church Mergers Work* with your staff and lay leaders. Engage your staff and lay leaders in the merger conversation. Discuss the pros and cons of merging with another church. Is this something your church should consider?

- *Find help.* Seek out a mentor, coach, or consultant to assist in facilitating the merger process. There is no need to pay the "stupid tax" that others have already paid. There are many landmines to step on and potholes to fall into on the merger journey. It is good stewardship and wise to have an experienced guide to assist you along the way. As wise King Solomon says, "Plans fail for lack of counsel, but with many advisers they succeed" (Prov. 15:22). Every church merger needs a facilitator that both congregations can trust who knows how to navigate the delicate conversations that have to occur for a successful merger.

- *Pray.* Intercede with an open heart that God will direct your steps and reveal merger possibilities if that will best serve his kingdom purpose for your church and your community. God spoke through his prophet Jeremiah telling his people in the Babylonian captivity to "seek the peace and prosperity of the city to which I have carried you into exile. Pray to the LORD for it, because if it prospers, you too will prosper" (Jer. 29:7). God said to Jonah, "Should I not have concern for the great city Nineveh, in which there are more than a hundred and twenty thousand people who cannot tell their right hand from their left?" (Jon. 4:11). God cares about the people in your region. Walk and pray around your community. Pray for God's burden for the lost and the least where he has planted your church. Ask God to show you where he is working in your community and then join him there with others who share your concern.

Bright Future Ahead

Healthy, mission-driven mergers are happening in an unprecedented way today. They are working with far more success than the more historically practiced ICU model. The big difference in these new kinds of mergers is

The idea of leveraging local church strengths to create ministry synergy is the core message of this book.

that they don't reduce church impact from two local churches down to one. Instead of diminishing kingdom presence and witness, they can gain greater influence, sometimes even multiplying it exponentially! The idea of leveraging local church strengths to create ministry synergy is the core message of this book. Rebirth, adoption, marriage, and even occasionally ICU mergers can and are succeeding and are worth considering. These new kinds of mergers offer another option besides holding on or dying. The idea of a healthy merger offers great hope and possibilities to the 80 percent of churches across the United States that are stuck, struggling, or declining.

Your church can flourish through merging with another. And if you're already a vibrant church that is growing, merging also offers a way to extend your reach and impact. This book is a guide on how to navigate successfully the merger journey for the strong and the struggling church.

Parker Hill Community Church in Scranton, Pennsylvania, was started in 1853 and Mark Stuenzi has been its lead pastor since 1989. During his many years there, he and his wife have built a number of relationships in the community, including relationships with believers in other churches. When a nearby church was struggling to find direction for its future, two key leaders from that church came to Mark and asked for some advice. Over a breakfast meeting, Mark encouraged them to consider a merger with another like-minded church. "I left the door open for the possibility that the 'adopting' church might be someone other than us, but also encouraged them to consider a relationship with us," he explains. A long process of what Mark calls "dating" followed that initial breakfast conversation. "Eventually, a merger was completed that totally changed our future as a church," Mark says.

Later Parker Hill welcomed another adoption, again with very positive results. "Both were real 'God things,'" he reports. "Both of the declining churches that we adopted have provided us with facilities and resources at just the right time. Our first adoption led us to adopt a multisite strategy and opened the door for much growth. Our second adoption provided us with a building for our student ministries at a time when they had outgrown their space. We were given a beautiful 150-year-old building—with only four parking spaces!" However, it was near enough to the main campus that parents could drop off and pick up their students conveniently.

The adoptions have given birth to much spiritual fruit already. For some, the Parker Hill adoptions have brought reconciliation through the healing of old wounds. Parker Hill's first merger was once a growing evangelical church. During a messy church split in the 1980s, many people who left that church ended up attending Parker Hill. The adoption process brought some of those people back together and brought a sense of closure to many who had left that church. "I know very personally how much that meant to at least one person," says Mark. "My wife had grown up in that church, came to Christ through a Vacation Bible School there, and was baptized in that sanctuary. There was a sense of closure for her."

For others it's given them hope. Harry was eighty years old when the first merger happened. He eventually became a sound technician in the children's ministry area. "It was great to see him serving every week—in his suit and tie—in a room that had previously been used only for the occasional potluck dinner," says Mark. "During his first week in this new role he was in tears because, as he told us, 'I never thought there would be so many children in this building again.'"

Parker Hill Community Church is all about helping people find the way back to God through Jesus Christ. The church's passion, according to Mark Stuenzi, "is to provide a spiritual home for people throughout northeast Pennsylvania." Church mergers have helped Parker Hill achieve that mission. "We will actively pursue this as a future strategy for outreach," Mark says.

Such is the promise and fruit of a Holy Spirit–guided, mission-focused merger. And today as never before, courageous, faith-directed leaders are exploring the possibility that a merger may be the vehicle that God uses to be *better together* in reaching more people, serving their communities better, and further extending the kingdom of God.

Two churches can be *better together* through a healthy merger! As we affirmed earlier, "Two are better than one because they have a good return for their labor" (Eccles. 4:9).

Is there a church merger on *your* horizon?

Appendix A

MERGER PROCESS CHECKLIST

Here is a brief to-do list to review as you go through the merger process. The chapters are identified for further explanation of each item.

- Clarify the mission and vision of your church. Why does your church exist—its mission? And what is it trying to accomplish—its vision? (Chapter Three)
- Assess the health of your church. Is it growing, plateaued, or declining? Are you strong, stable, stuck, or struggling? (Chapter One)
- Do a demographic survey of your community, perhaps using US Census Bureau data, Wikipedia, or a survey from Percept. (Chapter Fourteen)
- Assess the redemptive potential of your community. How many churches? How unchurched is the population? (Chapter Fourteen)
- Identify churches with merger potential. (Chapter Nine)
- Read this book with your board and staff. (Chapter Fourteen)
- Check with your denomination, association, or network for guidelines, resources, and opportunities around church mergers. (Chapter Nine)
- Find a mentor, coach, or consultant to assist you through the merger process. (Chapter Fourteen)

- Determine if your church is the lead or joining church. (Preface and Chapter One)

- Clarify the motive behind merging. Is it economic, facility, mission, multisite, reconciliation, or multiethnic driven? (Chapter Three)

- Determine which merger model best represents your merger opportunity. Is it a rebirth, adoption, marriage, or an ICU merger? (Chapter Two)

- Begin the merger conversation around the three questions that frame the merger process. Is this merger possible? Feasible? Desirable? (Chapter Four)

- Complete a church merger comparison profile. (Chapter Eleven)

- Create a timeline around the five stages of the merger process: dating, courtship, engagement, wedding, marriage. (Chapter Four)

- Address all merger issues and identify the potential deal breakers. (Chapter Twelve)

- Identify the potential landmines. (Chapter Six)

- Determine financial costs of the merger. (Chapter Seven)

- Define what a successful merger would look like one, three, and five years later. (Chapter Five)

- Determine the vote or poll process and what percentage is required for acceptance. (Chapters Four, Five, and Thirteen)

- Evaluate all ministries to determine integration, recalibration, or elimination. (Chapters Four and Eight)

- Create a communication strategy for both churches. (Chapters Four and Six)

- Develop the integration and implementation plan to commence on merger approval. (Chapters Four and Six)

- Plan the final celebration worship service and initial inaugural worship service. (Chapter Four)
- Prepare a legal document for church dissolution and transfer of property and assets on approval of the merger. (Chapter Seven)
- Confirm God's leading through prayer and unmistakable divinely orchestrated circumstances. (Chapter Nine)

Appendix B

EXAMPLE OF MERGER ISSUES TO RESOLVE

Here is an excellent example of how the two churches in Chapter Twelve addressed the twenty-five issues every church merger needs to discuss. It is very thorough and a helpful template for churches working through the feasibility stage of merger deliberations.

Doctrinal

Theological Beliefs

Sun Valley and Bethany have very compatible historic orthodox, evangelical, theological beliefs. The one distinction is that Sun Valley views pastors as being a type of elder, therefore, the title of pastor is reserved for men only.

Governance

The structure of leadership in the constitution and bylaws of both churches is very similar in this respect. However, Sun Valley's practice and interpretation has been "staff-led, board-protected," whereas Bethany's present practice is "elder-led." Sun Valley Community Church is led by the executive team, which consists of the lead pastors, campus pastors, and select executive-level staff members. The board of servant leaders is constituted by up to nine leaders, the majority of which are lay leaders selected from all campuses, in addition to the lead pastors. Lay servant leaders may serve up to two three-year terms. The staff work for the lead pastors while the lead pastors work at the pleasure of the board of servant leaders.

In the merger with Bethany, two or three leaders from the Bethany campus will be selected and trained to join the board of servant leaders.

Affiliations

Sun Valley is an independent church that chooses to align with the association of churches called Converge Worldwide. We own our own property, choose our own leaders, and determine our own visions, values, and distribution of our assets. We plan to continue that alliance after the merger.

Philosophy of Ministry

Mission, Vision, and Values

Every local body of believers exists for the great commission "make disciples of all nations" by living out the great commandment "love God and love people." Sun Valley and Bethany are no different.

Sun Valley's vision is to be a life-changing, family-centered, community-impacting, world-reaching church. We do this by reliance on God's word and his Holy Spirit. We train our staff to be volunteer specialists who envision and equip our members to make an impact in their families, neighborhood, church, community, and world. As a church we are committed to sending missionaries, planting churches, and multisiting congregations while training other churches to do the same. We give strong support to all who choose to trust God in these endeavors.

Sun Valley's mission statement is, "Helping each other move toward authentic Christian living." This statement captures our stated values of "authenticity, community, and generosity." We work diligently to see these values lived out by every person who calls Sun Valley his or her church home.

Strategy

Individuals are encouraged to follow a pathway described as "Come-Grow-Serve-Go," highlighting the goals of experiencing God in the weekend services, growing in relationships and understanding of the Word through small-group communities, serving one another in meaningful ministry, and going out into the world to make a difference. This is very similar to Bethany's "Get in—Get together—Get out—Get serving." We have a commitment to share what we know with other like-minded churches around the valley, state, country, and world.

Worship Style

Our worship style is decidedly contemporary. However, we understand that the makeup of the Gilbert campus lends itself to that style. We recognize the need to consider the makeup of the Bethany campus and plan to be sensitive to the needs of the significant number of long-term Bethany attendees who prefer a traditional style.

Preaching

The weekend teaching will be live on the Bethany campus, and the Sun Valley–Gilbert campus will have a mixture of live and video. As we add more services to the Bethany campus, those services may be live or video, based on what is best for the overall ministry of Sun Valley.

Membership

Sun Valley's requirements for membership are as follows: (1) believer in Christ, (2) baptized after conversion, (3) attended Starting Point [their new member class], (4) active in a small group (or faith community), (5) serving in a ministry, and (6) completed membership covenant approved by the board.

These requirements are similar to Bethany's but convey a greater expectation that members will actively participate in the body life of the church. Sun Valley places great value on its members knowing and living the vision, mission, and methods of the ministry.

After listening to the members of Bethany and prayer-fully considering this adoption, the leaders of Sun Valley have agreed to amend the bylaws of Sun Valley to allow all current Bethany members to be "grandfathered" into the membership of Sun Valley. "Grandfathered" members will be encouraged to attend a Sun Valley Starting Point presentation in order to clearly understand how Sun Valley sees its members living out the vision, mission, and methods of ministry they promote.

Programs

All programs will be evaluated on both campuses from the same criterion. Concerns about faith communities have been addressed in previous conversations. All programs must fit in a category of Come-Grow-Serve-Go. It is our practice to re-evaluate every program on a yearly basis to make sure that it is accomplishing its goal.

Budget

We are one church . . . one vision, one leadership team, one budget, one staff, and one bank account. Giving, budgets, and current account balances from Sun Valley and Bethany will be combined and managed by the Sun Valley church administrator, executive team, and board of servant leaders to address the needs and mission of all campuses.

Personnel

Expectations

This merger is an "adoption," which is defined as "a stable or stuck church that is integrated under the vision of a stronger, vibrant, and typically larger church." In this scenario, Sun Valley is the leading church and Bethany is the joining church.

Senior Pastor

Scott Ridout and Chad Moore share the lead pastor role at Sun Valley and will assume that role for the Bethany campus as well.

Boards and Committees

The elder board will be replaced by one central board of servant leaders (all of whom must still qualify according to 1 Timothy 3 and Titus 1, like our elders). This board consists of the lead pastors and a large majority of lay members selected as representatives from all campuses. Local campus leadership will be led primarily by the executive staff team of that campus under the leadership of a central executive team, which consists of the campus pastors, lead pastors, and selected executive team members from different campuses.

Sun Valley does not use committees but does have task forces. Committees that serve in an area of ministry focus (such as missions) will come under the supervision of the staff over that area. The staff and board of Sun Valley have the power to assign task forces to tackle issues they deem important, but not necessarily the primary focus of the staff and board (e.g., the building task force on the Gilbert campus). All other committees at Bethany that are not converted to staff or board-assigned task forces will be phased out.

In addition, Sun Valley will add three current Bethany elder board members to Sun Valley's elder board from a recommended list of five.

Staff

We are committed to retain and train the existing Bethany staff, provided that giving on the Bethany campus can support this commitment. Pay and benefit packages will be examined and will come into alignment within the standard ranges of Sun Valley in or prior to 2012.

Missionaries

The same commitment that has been given to the staff is being given to Bethany's missionaries. Missionaries will not be penalized for duplication on both campuses. Like all staff and ministries, all missions and missionary emphases are subject to evaluation.

Legal

Church Name

Sun Valley Community Church–Bethany campus. We will adopt the name Sun Valley Community Church, but will be known as the "Bethany campus" to honor our heritage. Sun Valley has a great and growing name recognition in our valley and it makes sense to keep that name. In written form we will identify that campus as "Bethany-Tempe" so that people not familiar with Bethany can know the location of the campus.

Voting

Although the Gilbert campus needs no congregational vote, we will do a confirmation vote. Our understanding is that the Bethany campus needs to have a congregational approval by three-fourths of members present. This vote will not only make Scott Ridout and Chad Moore lead pastors at Bethany, but it will also replace the constitution and bylaws of Bethany Community Church with the constitution and bylaws of Sun Valley Community Church.

Property and Facility

Sun Valley's expressed plan is not only to keep the campus but also to maximize its use for kingdom impact. The Bethany campus is one of the most strategically located campuses in Phoenix. Our vision for Tempe-Chandler-Ahwatukee is unwavering. Most likely we will have a campaign for campus renovation and deferred maintenance within the first year of the adoption. Sun Valley will assume ownership of all property of Bethany Community Church.

Assets and Liabilities

We have sent our information to Bethany. We would like to see the information on the Bethany Community Church property, the Bethany Learning Center, the $1.0 million deferred maintenance needs, the missionary house in Mesa, and any other property that Bethany may own. Sun Valley will work with the leadership of the Bethany elders to work out the best possible scenario for handling the assets and liabilities of Bethany Community Church with integrity.

Debt Management

We have sent our information to Bethany. We have handled our debt with integrity. We have $10.5 million in debt—$9.5 million on Building A, $1.0 on Building B. We will not take on any more debt on the Gilbert campus and, in fact, have completed the downstairs children's area (about 20,000 square feet) debt free.

Timeline

We suggest the following timeline, which was suggested by John Wood from Bethany:

- August 7: Make the adoption announcement.
- Next six weeks: Host a number of town halls and discussions to answer questions and dream the possibilities of our future. (We suggest having Chad Moore and Scott Ridout speak on several weekend services during that time.)

- September 25: Take a congregational vote.
- October 9: Host a celebration service commemorating the years of great ministry God has given us as a church.
- October 16: Have the first service as Sun Valley Community Church–Bethany campus.

Appendix C

FAQs EXAMPLE FROM BETHANY-SUN VALLEY CHURCHES

This document shows an effective list of FAQs that was created after each church addressed the merger issues at stake (and that were listed in Appendix B). It explains how the merger conversation began, the benefits of merging, the merger process with a timeline, voting guidelines, and specific guidance to each member. It also models a nondenominational church joining a denominational church.

Bethany-Sun Valley FAQs

How did this all come about?

In fall 2010, Scott Ridout and Chad Moore, the lead pastors of Sun Valley Community Church, initiated a conversation with Rich Hendrix to let him know of their plans to start a campus in the West Chandler–Tempe area. Instead of starting work from scratch, they asked Rich if Bethany would consider joining forces to become one church. After many conversations between these leaders, a dialogue began with the elders of Bethany. Initially, Bethany's elders made the decision not to pursue this option. However, with Rich's resignation in March, the elders restarted the conversation with Sun Valley, resolved some earlier misunderstanding, and, with the prayer support of Sun Valley's leaders, began to wrestle through the best scenario for the future of Bethany. After numerous meetings, discussions, and lots of prayer seeking God's will, both leadership teams agreed to hire Jim Tomberlin from Multi-site Solutions to explore the feasibility and desirability of our two churches becoming one through what can best be described as an "adoption" process.

Who is Sun Valley Community Church?

Sun Valley Community Church began in 1990 with a vision to reach the East Valley and beyond. Since that time Sun Valley and its leaders have parented or partnered in the start of twenty-eight churches in Arizona and Southern California. In addition they are a leading church in the collaboration efforts between churches in the state of Arizona. Sun Valley's stated purpose is to "help each other move toward authentic Christian living" and champions the values of "authenticity, community, and generosity." God has used the ministry of Sun Valley to effectively touch the lives of a very wide range of people from all backgrounds and ages—young and old, churched and unchurched, mature Christians and new believers. Over twelve hundred people have been baptized at Sun Valley since 2009 and hundreds have been sent on overseas mission trips as well.

Currently, weekend attendance at the Gilbert campus hovers around 3,600, which is near the maximum capacity of that campus. A second campus will open this fall in Casa Grande to minister to that community.

What are some of the unique similarities between Bethany and Sun Valley?

Bethany and Sun Valley share the same vision: to help Christians come to full maturity in Christ while making an impact on the lives of those outside the church, both locally and globally. Our congregations are full of people who are seeking meaningful community with one another while influencing the community outside the four walls of the church through generous living and giving. Our doctrinal statements are compatible and our commitment to the word of God is uncompromised. For years, our student and children's ministries have worked together for camps and other events. Mission emphases shared by the two churches include Streetlight, Helping Hands, IHELP, and the Husa family in Papua New Guinea. Our leadership teams have met and found that we are "united in spirit, intent on one purpose."

What are the benefits of this "adoption"?

Simply put, we are better together than we could ever be apart. Both churches bring much to the table. Each ministry brings a commitment to the word of God in our lives and the work of God in our communities. Both bring a heart for families and the next generation while wanting to honor those who have brought us to where we are thus far. Both have a vibrant local and foreign missions emphasis. We are motivated, gifted people who want to honor God by using our gifts and abilities to advance God's purposes. Coming together as one church will bring a synergy to our ministry—using the best of both congregations to launch us toward our one goal of knowing Christ and making Him known.

There are several benefits for Bethany in this adoption. The greatest benefit is the leadership that has proven itself in the ministry of Sun Valley. We believe Sun Valley's leadership, vision, implementation, systems, and structures will enhance and maximize the impact of the ministry of the people of Bethany on our campus, in the community, and around the world. An additional benefit is that we expect a very quick influx of trained and willing volunteers who have attended at Sun Valley but live closer to Bethany.

How will the campuses work together?

Each campus will have a dedicated campus pastor who will work with a staff team and volunteer leaders on that particular campus; all campuses will be assisted by a central support team; will be guided by one vision, one ministry model, one budget; and led by one executive team, protected by one board of servant leaders with representatives from all campuses.

What remains the same?

Much that is already at Bethany will be the same. We continue on the same campus, with the same people, having the same loving spirit and the same commitment to God. We will experience vibrant weekend services focused on God's word, develop meaningful relationships through faith communities, and maintain our local and global mission emphasis. Initially we will continue with one service but as we grow we will be able to add additional services with differentiated worship styles.

What is going to change?

You will notice some changes immediately. Bethany will adopt Sun Valley's ministry names and pathways. We will also use Sun Valley's staff titles so that leaders who perform the same roles on different campuses can be easily identified.

Sun Valley has been very successful at attracting young families, both churched and unchurched, so one of the biggest changes you should notice is the addition of new people. The Bethany campus will also experience new ministries that Sun Valley has developed for many walks of life including family, marriage, and young adults.

What is the role of women at Sun Valley?

Women are an important and integral part of the ministry. Women hold a number of leadership positions in the church. All servants, men and women, are asked to lead and teach based on their gifting. Sun Valley holds that both their pastors and servant leaders (equivalent of elder at Bethany) must meet all qualifications of eldership as outlined in 1 Timothy 3 and Titus 1. As such, the title of pastor is equated with elder and is only given to men. Women can hold any position in the church except servant leader or pastor. Women leaders can be licensed for ministry.

Who will be our senior pastor(s)?

Scott Ridout and Chad Moore, who share the lead pastor role at Sun Valley, will take on that role for the Bethany campus as well. Scott and Chad bring a strong complement of strengths to the lead pastor position. Scott brings great strategic and implementation skills and Chad brings strong communication and visionary skills. Together they bring a great balanced and wide foundation for our future leadership.

How will Sunday services be done?

The Sunday service will be live and in person on the Bethany campus and services on the Sun Valley–Gilbert campus will have a mixture of live and video teaching. Although Sun Valley uses a contemporary style in their services on the Gilbert campus, they have plans to implement a traditional service as a part of future expansion on the Bethany campus. In the beginning we will continue to have one service and add a second service as the attendance grows. The leaders of Sun Valley are keenly aware of the large number of people on the Bethany campus who prefer a traditional worship service. They recognize the desire of many to have a service that is solely "traditional" in style although many others would prefer a service that is solely "contemporary" in style. As we add more services to the Bethany campus, those services may be live or video, based on what is best for the overall ministry of the combined campuses of Sun Valley.

What will be the name of our church?

Sun Valley Community Church—Bethany Campus. We will adopt the name Sun Valley Community Church, but will be known as the "Bethany Campus" to honor our heritage. Sun Valley has a great and growing name recognition in our valley and it makes sense to keep that name. In written form we will identify our campus as "Bethany-Tempe" so that people not familiar with Bethany can know the location of our campus.

What will happen to my membership?

Sun Valley's requirements for membership are as follows: (1) believer in Christ, (2) baptized after conversion, (3) attended Starting Point classes, (4) active in a small group (or faith community), (5) serving in a ministry, and (6) completed membership covenant approved by the board. Sun Valley places great value on its members knowing and living the vision, mission, and methods of the ministry. Present Bethany members and attendees will have a number of opportunities in the first few months to continue their membership by walking through the Sun Valley Starting Point presentation and by completing the membership application process.

What will happen to the campus?

Sun Valley's plan is to maximize the use of the Bethany campus for greater kingdom impact. The Bethany campus is one of the most strategically located campuses in Phoenix. Families who currently attend the Sun Valley–Gilbert campus, but who live in the Tempe-Chandler-Ahwatukee area, will be encouraged to worship on the Bethany campus. You will also see facility improvements as we begin to catch up on delayed maintenance and upgrade projects.

What will happen to existing leadership teams (e.g., elders, staff, etc.)?

Bethany's elder board will be replaced by one central Sun Valley board of servant leaders (all of whom must qualify according to 1 Timothy 3 and Titus 1, like our elders). The servant leader board includes both of the lead pastors and a number of lay leaders selected from all of the church's campuses and will include Bethany representation. Local campus leadership will be led primarily by the campus executive staff team under the leadership of a central executive team over all campuses. This central executive team will consist of the various campus pastors, the lead pastors, and selected executive team members from different campuses.

Sun Valley has communicated a commitment to "retain and train" Bethany's existing staff, provided that giving on the Bethany campus can support this commitment. The same commitment has been given for our missionaries. Giving, budgets, and current account balances from Sun Valley and Bethany will be combined and managed by the Sun Valley church administrator, executive team, and board of servant leaders to address the needs and mission of all campuses.

Is this "one church—multisite" a risky new approach? Does it work?

Since the mid-1990s more than three thousand churches have pioneered this concept. Studies show that 90 percent of all multisite ventures are successful. God is blessing this movement within US churches. Although the details vary, several local Phoenix area churches have successfully adopted the multisite concept: East Valley Bible Church and Praxis became Redemption Church (three campuses), Word of Grace and Citichurch became City of Grace (two campuses), and Central Christian has added campuses and adopted Crosspoint Church in Glendale. We have hired a well-known expert on multisite, Jim Tomberlin, a resident of Phoenix, to guide us through this process.

What is the financial status of both churches?

As with most fast-growing churches, Sun Valley has financed new buildings to support growth. However, the portion of its income used for debt service (approximately 30 percent) is in line with limits recommended in church-lending literature, its lenders are happy with where things stand, all loans are current, no payments have ever been missed, and its annual income is growing year over year. In addition, it is in the middle of a capital campaign that will further pay down some of the debt as well as add value to the Gilbert campus. In comparison, Bethany has paid off its debts during the course of many years. However, our focus of investing in ministry over facilities for many years has left us with an increasingly urgent need to invest nearly $1,000,000 in roof and air conditioner replacements and parking lot repairs. The elder board and the leaders of Sun Valley feel that these needs can be accommodated by the future growth of our campus. Although finances should always be a consideration in any union, the true motivation for this union is kingdom and community impact, bringing the strengths of both ministries under one leadership team.

Why have the elders recommended this adoption?

We believe that the best days of ministry through Bethany are ahead of us. We have always viewed ourselves as being a people of great faith and we believe that God is leading us in this partnership. Sun Valley has tremendous momentum as a church and has invited us to join forces with them in order to reach the East Valley with the good news of Jesus Christ. Our future impact in Tempe-Chandler-Ahwatukee is dependent on clear vision, strong leadership, and personal obedience to follow God as a people of faith. We believe that God has presented us with this opportunity to join a very successful work in progress.

What is the procedure and timeline for this adoption?

From the announcement on July 17 to the vote on September 25, we will host a number of town halls and discussions to answer questions and dream the possibilities of our future. Chad Moore and Scott Ridout will preach during Sunday services several times during that time and attend some of the town halls. On September 25, 2011, the members of Bethany will vote. If 75 percent or more of the voting members approve the elders' recommendation to merge with Sun Valley, the merger will be completed. If the vote confirms the elder board recommendation we will host a celebration service commemorating the rich history of great ministry God has given us as a church on October 2, 2011. Then on October 9, 2011, we will mark our new beginning and the first service as Sun Valley Community Church–Bethany Campus!

What happens to Bethany Community Church if the vote passes?

Although the legal details remain to be worked out, the church would donate the Bethany assets and liabilities to Sun Valley Community Church as provided for in Bethany's articles of incorporation. We would then begin operating as the Bethany campus of Sun Valley Community Church as one body joined together under the Sun Valley Constitution and bylaws (which have been posted to the Bethany website for your review). At the appropriate time, Bethany's nonprofit 501c(3) corporate shell would be dissolved. This process will make us one church with one vision operating in multiple locations.

What happens if the vote does not pass?

Regardless of the outcome of the members' vote, Bethany needs to change. As witnessed by our lack of healthy growth over many years, the current status of Bethany is not God's will. If the membership votes that merger with Sun Valley is not God's will for Bethany then the senior pastor search committee, which has already developed a profile for our next senior pastor, will launch immediately into a search for him. We expect the search to take at least several months and potentially eighteen to twenty-four months to find the right pastor. In the meantime, we would continue with an interim pastor to carefully manage our finances and adjust our budget and staffing as needed. We would also start making changes in our structure to refocus on reaching the local community more effectively.

What should I do now?

First and foremost seek God's will for Bethany. Change is coming to Bethany and it can be a difficult challenge; we ask that you do the following:

- *Celebrate* the wonderful opportunity God has presented to our congregation!

- *Pray* for the leadership and staff as they work out the details of a possible adoption.
- *Explore* the possibilities with Sun Valley by attending weekend worship services and the town halls.
- *Seek* God's will for the future of Bethany and its impact on his kingdom.
- *Vote on September 25* to acknowledge what you believe to be God's will for us.

Appendix D

FAQs EXAMPLE FROM GINGHAMSBURG CHURCH

Ginghamsburg Church (see Systematic God Checks in Chapter 9) does a good job at anticipating the typical questions a joining church will have as it enters a merger. Notice how Ginghamsburg addresses with clarity and confidence what will change, pastor leadership, governance, membership, finances, adult Sunday school classes, and name change.

Ginghamsburg Church FAQs

Will our worship service change?
The gospel message will never change but media and music will transform into what will best connect with the multicultural community surrounding Ft. McKinley. We will become missionaries to the community, willing to give up our own preferences as consumers of what the church offers so that we might be producers of blessings within the lives of others.

How will our congregation look different if we merge?
This summer, Ginghamsburg will identify twenty or so "mission" families from its current congregation who will leave the Tipp City campus to worship and serve at the Ft. McKinley campus. The goal is to create a contagious community that will attract into the Ft. McKinley congregation those who live in the surrounding neighborhoods.

Will a pastor be appointed to Ft. McKinley?
The leadership team of Ginghamsburg Church will hold a nationwide search to identify a campus pastor. This individual,

once selected, will be appointed to Ginghamsburg Church and will be part of Ginghamsburg's pastoral team under the leadership of senior pastor Mike Slaughter and executive pastor Sue Nilson Kibbey. This pastor will be stationed at Ft. McKinley to facilitate worship at the Ft. McKinley campus as well as to oversee and lead the day-to-day ministry of the Ft. McKinley campus and its facilities.

When will the new campus pastor start?
Once this pastor is identified, he or she will serve initially for up to six months at the Ginghamsburg main campus to be immersed in the ministry practices, leadership strategies, and mission-driven DNA of Ginghamsburg. As this mentoring period is in process, a pastoral team of three people, including John Ward, will provide pastoral care and teaching at the Ft. McKinley campus.

Will the current Ft. McKinley lay leadership teams be retained (e.g., trustees, staff-parish relations, etc.)?
No. As one unified church, the Ginghamsburg and Ft. McKinley campuses will fall under the authority of the one unified Ginghamsburg Church leadership board. This board provides all of the oversight functions required by the United Methodist Book of Discipline. People from Ft. McKinley will be eligible for future participation in this board if they meet the requirements: church membership; demonstrated commitment to serving in front-line ministry, faithful worship attendance, and the 10 percent biblical tithe; and an interview with and approval by the current leadership board. The campus pastor will attend all leadership board meetings to provide the Ft. McKinley campus needs. The campus pastor will also identify a campus logistics team at Ft. McKinley to help with campus facility management.

I am a member of Ft. McKinley. Will I retain my membership?
If you are currently a member in good standing of Ft. McKinley, your membership will transfer automatically into membership

at Ginghamsburg Church. If you are not already a member of Ft. McKinley, you or anyone who wishes to join the church from the point of merger forward must complete the membership process as currently defined by Ginghamsburg Church. That process includes attending the twelve-week follower's life class, an interview with a class facilitator, and a commitment to demonstrate the Ginghamsburg mission.

How will I have a voice in what happens after the merger?

Members are encouraged to share their input, feedback, and wisdom with the pastoral staff and leadership board through a variety of forums. For example, each spring and fall, senior pastor Mike Slaughter meets with the "kingdom investors" of the church, those who invest their time and financial resources into the mission of the church, to deliver a "state of the union" address, cast vision for the future, and solicit feedback. However, decisions about ministry and mission are made by the leadership team as directed by the Holy Spirit. Decisions are not made by consensus, majority rule, or committee vote.

Will we still have Sunday school classes?

Yes. Over time, all areas of discipleship will expand beyond what exists today, starting initially with children's programming. Classes for all ages will eventually be offered not only on Sunday mornings as they are now but also at several alternative times throughout the week.

What will happen to Ft. McKinley's current mission outreach programs such as the food pantry, GED program, and so on?

Ft. McKinley's mission outreach will become part of New Path Ministries, under the direction of New Path director Marcia Florkey. (New Path is the 501c[3] outreach arm of Ginghamsburg Church that encompasses its food, car, furniture, clothing, and medical equipment ministries.) Marcia will evaluate current Ft. McKinley outreach programs for impact and effectiveness and identify those to be merged into existing New Path initiatives or expanded.

What will happen to the Ft. McKinley budget, our current funds, and future giving?

Giving, budgets, and current account balances from Ft. McKinley and Ginghamsburg Church will be combined and managed by the Ginghamsburg chief stewardship officer, senior management team, and leadership board to address the needs and mission of all campuses.

Will we keep the Ft. McKinley name?

This is to be determined. The current intent is to develop a name and signage that will reflect both Ginghamsburg and Ft. McKinley. Current ideas under consideration include the "Ft. McKinley" Ginghamsburg Campus, Ft. McKinley—a Ginghamsburg Church community, and Ginghamsburg at the Fort.

What happens if we vote "no" on the merger?

If the merger is voted down, the Ginghamsburg leadership team will consider it as a sign of God's protection that neither Ginghamsburg nor Ft. McKinley should go in this direction. Both will remain two separate churches. Senior pastor Mike Slaughter will be removed as the appointed pastor to Ft. McKinley. With the exception of the clubhouse ministry targeted for June at Ft. McKinley, all current partnership activities will cease including speakers for the pulpit, music, and any other programming interfaces. This will free up both Ginghamsburg and Ft. McKinley to pursue new partnerships and other ministry directions.

Appendix E

FAQs EXAMPLE FROM WOODSIDE BIBLE CHURCH

Here is another basic FAQ template used by Woodside Bible Church in Royal Oak, Michigan (profiled in Chapter Four), a congregation with considerable experience in mergers. Notice how Woodside explains why they are merging.

Woodside Bible FAQs

What does a "merger" mean?
We will become one congregation known as Woodside Bible Church. The church would become a Woodside Bible Church campus governed by the Woodside elder board. [NAMES] will serve as campus pastors part time to care for the campus. We would be one church meeting at several locations. The campus will use Woodside's current constitution, statement of faith, and missions' policies as its governing documents. All current members of [JOINING CHURCH'S NAME] will be given the opportunity to automatically become members of Woodside.

Who will preach each Sunday?
Like the other campuses, we would have a teaching team that would preach the message. Primarily [NAMES] will comprise the team. The message content is the same across all campuses.

Will there be ministry opportunities at the new campus?
There will be many opportunities to prayerfully consider. Volunteers will be needed in worship leading, children's ministry, small groups, students, young adults, and so on. We will

welcome those who have a desire to be part of building this new campus in [CITY].

What are the financial liabilities?

Members of our finance committee have studied this proposal and are excited about the possibilities of what God can do in the city of Royal Oak. The church is debt free and brings approximately $[AMOUNT] in savings. The church also owns a parsonage that is mortgage free. The building is in excellent condition and is located at [ADDRESS]. It is our plan to cover our weekly expenses from the current level of giving.

What would happen to [NAME OF JOINING CHURCH'S] staff and volunteers?

All paid church staff will be evaluated by [NAME OF CHURCH] deacons and Woodside elders and, if appropriate, be offered roles within the Woodside team. [NAME OF CHURCH] ministry leaders will be given the opportunity to serve at the Royal Oak campus in their areas of passion and giftedness.

Why are we doing this merger?

The merger fits into our vision at Woodside: Helping people belong to Christ, join in Christ, grow in Christ, and reach the world for Christ. Our discussion with the leadership of [JOINING CHURCH'S NAME] began in [DATE] and has involved much prayer and interaction. The merger will allow us to join forces with the wonderful people of [JOINING CHURCH'S NAME] in reaching the Royal Oak region for Christ. As leadership we know that this church is God's and we want to serve Him. Let's together be dependent on God in prayer and express our confidence in Him by boldly acting in faith.

What are the steps in concluding the merger?

The congregation of [JOINING CHURCH'S NAME] and the congregation of Woodside Bible Church—all campuses—will vote Saturday and Sunday [DATES]. If the vote passes, the legal work will be completed, launch date selected, and the specifics of campus development will begin. We will be inviting people to join us in developing another Woodside campus, helping us realize our vision of affecting our region with the life-changing message of Jesus Christ. Meetings will take place early in October for people to get more information on the service opportunities at Royal Oak.

Appendix F

FAQs ON PREPARING FOR A MERGER VOTE

Most church mergers involve a congregational vote or poll of both churches. Regardless of the church polity, it is recommended that a congregational vote or poll be taken to cement the congregation's sense of ownership in a merger decision. Because people will vote with their feet and checkbook, it's better to know before the merger how the congregation really feels about it. Here is a good example of the questions to address in preparing a congregation for the merger vote. It was excerpted and adapted with permission from a 2011 document created by Crossroads Church, Ruston, Louisiana.

What will the voting process look like on September 18?

Each church will gather individually. The attached ballot will be passed out along with an envelope and it will then be returned when completed and signed. The elders will collect the ballots and confidentially review them. After the votes of all members are counted, a report of the results will be provided to both churches as soon as practical. An absentee process will be used for those who know they cannot be present on September 18, and the details of this absentee process will be communicated to both churches on September 7.

Will I have a chance to ask additional questions before the vote?

Yes. Both churches will hold their own family meetings up to two weeks before the vote on September 18 when questions can be asked in large-group settings as well as submitted privately on cards. In addition the elders are always available to visit with you or with your small group to make sure everyone's questions are answered in full.

What vote is required to approve the merger?

Both churches must say "yes" before there can be a merger. If both churches vote 51 percent or more in favor of the merger (a majority "yes" vote at each church), then a merger is permissible. The question then becomes, "Is a merger wise?" The elders will provide their decision on the wisdom of pursuing a merger once the complete votes are reviewed, and this decision will be provided at the same time the results of the vote are reported to both churches.

What if both churches decide to pursue a strategic merger?

If the elders and membership of both churches decide to pursue a strategic merger, then we will begin an implementation period in the months following the vote. Practically, we would begin meeting as one church on October 2 but there are legal aspects of the merger that will take some additional time to complete.

What if either church votes "no" to the merger?

If either church votes "no" to the merger, then the churches will not merge. In that event—whether you vote "yes" or "no" on your ballot—you will remain a member of your current church under the leadership of the current elders at that church. Each church will then proceed independently of the other.

Appendix G

CHURCHES NAMED

Church Name	City, State	Pastor or Leader	Website	Chapter
Austin New Church	Austin, TX	Brandon Hatmaker	www.austinnewchurch.com	9
Bay Area Fellowship	Corpus Christi, TX	Bil Cornelius	www.bayareafellowship.com	1
Bear Valley Church	Lakewood, CO	Jim Walters	www.bvchurch.org	1
Calvary Christian Church	Winchester, KY	Brian Walton	www.calvarychristian.net	10
Capstone Church	Anderson, SC	David Barfield	www.capstonechurch.com	9
Central Baptist Bearden	Knoxville, TN	Larry Fields (senior pastor), Robert Bowman, (associate pastor)	www.cbcbearden.org	7
Chelsea Community Church	Chelsea, AL	Greg Davis	www.chelseacc.com	8
Christ Community Church	Ruston, LA	Len Woods	www.cccruston.com	3
Church of the Highlands	Birmingham, AL	Chris Hodges	http://churchofthehighlands.com/	14
Coral Ridge Presbyterian Church	Ft. Lauderdale, FL	Tullian Tchividjian	www.coralridge.org	2
Crossroads Church	Ruston, LA	Wade Burnett	Not available yet	3
Eagle Brook Church	Centerville, MN	Bob Merritt	www.eaglebrookchurch.com	1
Fellowship Bible Church	Little Rock, AR	Mark Henry	www.fbclr.com	3

Church	Location	Pastor	Website	
First West Church	West Monroe, LA	John Avant	www.firstwest.cc	2
Ginghamsburg Church	Tipp City, OH	Michael Slaughter	www.ginghamsburg.org	9
Granger Community Church	Granger, IN	Mark Beeson	www.gccwired.com	3
Healing Place Church	Baton Rouge, LA	Dino Rizzo	www.healingplacechurch.org	3
LifeChurch.tv	Edmond, OK	Craig Groeschel	www.lifechurch.tv	1, 9
Lowell Assembly of God	Tewksbury, MA	Richard Bertrand, (senior pastor), Frank Rondon (associate pastor)	www.lowellag.org	8
Mariners Church	Irvine, CA	Kenton Beshore	www.marinerschurch.org	3
Mars Hill Church	Seattle, WA	Mark Driscoll	www.marshillchurch.org	1
Mosaic Church	Little Rock, AR	Mark DeYmaz	www.mosaicchurch.net	3
New Hope Church	Wooster, OH	Tim Broughton	www.mynewhope.tv	3
New Life Church	Meriden, CT	Will Marotti	www.innewlife.com	5
New Life Community Church	Chicago, IL	Mark Jobe	www.newlifechicago.org	1, 3
North Point Community Church	Alpharetta, GA	Andy Stanley	www.northpoint.org	1
Parker Hill Community Church	Scranton, PA	Mark Stuenzi	www.parkerhill.org	14

(Continued)

Church Name	City, State	Pastor or Leader	Website	Chapter
Quest Church	Seattle, WA	Eugene Cho	www.seattlequest.org	4
Redemption Church	Tempe, AZ	Justin Anderson	www.redemptionaz.com	1, 13
Silver Creek Fellowship	Silverton, OR	Rob Barnes	www.silvercreekfellowship.org	10
Sun Valley Community Church	Gilbert, AZ	Scott Ridout, Chad Moore (co-pastors)	www.sunvalleycc.com	12, 13
The Chapel	Akron, OH	Paul Sartarelli	www.the-chapel.org	6
The Chapel in Grayslake	Libertyville, IL	Scott Chapman, Jeff Griffin (co-pastors)	www.chapel.org	1, 10
Vintage Faith Church	Santa Cruz, CA	Dan Kimball		9
Washington Heights	Ogden, UT	Roy Gruber	www.theheightscommunity.org	2
Woodside Bible Church	Troy, MI	Doug Schmidt	www.woodsidebible.org	4

Appendix H

MERGER RESEARCH

Leadership Network Phone Survey

Leadership Network commissioned a phone survey among a random sample of senior pastors of Protestant churches. A total of 605 pastors participated. The survey occurred in December 2007. The data were collected around the following objectives: to ascertain the percent of churches that have merged with another congregation in the past three years, to determine the percent of churches that have seriously discussed a merger in the last year, and to examine the likelihood churches will merge within the next two years. A merger was defined as multiple congregations joining together to form a single congregation. Primary findings include the following:

- Two percent had merged in the last three years.
- Five percent had discussed merging during the last year (and an additional 2 percent had discussed sharing their facilities with another congregation as a possible step toward a merger).
- Among the 5 percent that had discussed merging in the next two years, a fourth (24 percent) said they continue to move toward a merger ("definitely" or "probably"), and the rest said they're not likely to merge (71 percent) or they didn't know (5 percent).

Leadership Network Online Survey

Leadership Network used blogs and other public announcements to publicize a fifty-question survey that ran from March 3 to May 10, 2011. We received 430 responses to the survey, but did most of the analysis with 151 churches that (1) are from the United States and Canada, (2) have already experienced a merger, and (3) completed the majority of the survey. Select results were published as *Making Multisite Mergers Work: New Options for Being One Church in Two or More Locations* by Warren Bird and Kristin Walters.[1]

A summary of the merger survey learnings are in Chapter Three.

Outside Surveys That Mention Mergers

- U.S. Congregational Life Survey, www.uscongregations.org
- Faith Communities Today Survey, www.faithcommunities today.org
- Megachurches Today Survey, www.hartfordinstitute.org

Acknowledgments

Our list of the world's most supportive people begins with Jim's wife, Deryl, and Warren's wife, Michelle. We love doing life together with you.

We also thank the patient churches that helped us learn how to be pastors. Jim credits Hoffmantown Baptist Church, Albuquerque, New Mexico; Faith Baptist Church, Kaiserslautern, Germany; Woodmen Valley Chapel, Colorado Springs, Colorado; and Willow Creek Community Church, Chicago, Illinois. Warren wants to single out two: First Baptist, Atlanta, Georgia; and Princeton Alliance Church, Princeton, New Jersey, the latter where Warren was on staff for eleven years.

Jim also expresses appreciation to the hundreds of churches who have "survived" his consulting—and who have taught him valuable insights from the front trenches of ministry. Warren likewise appreciates all the pastoral leaders who have welcomed his visits and interviews through Leadership Network and through his previous work with the Charles E. Fuller Institute for Evangelism and Church Growth under Carl George and also the Beeson Institute for Advanced Church Leadership under Dale Galloway.

This book would not have happened without Warren's excellent support staff, especially Kelly Kulesza and Stephanie Plagens at Leadership Network, as well as other colleagues there: Dave Travis, Greg Ligon, and Mark Sweeney. Staff at Jossey-Bass who helped improve this book include Sheryl Fullerton, Joanne Clapp Fullagar, Alison Knowles, Lisa Coronado-Morse, and Susan Geraghty.

We also got help from several specialists including Marc Glassman, a statistical consultant; Scott Thumma, researcher and statistician; and attorneys Wendi Hodges and David Middlebrook, who carefully reviewed the legal material in Chapter Seven.

Warren's prayer partner for this project was Len Kageler and Jim's ministry-long prayer partner is Becky Kennard.

Many people read the manuscript and suggested important and helpful improvements: Ed Bahler, Russ Bredholt, Charlie Boyd, Wade Burnett, Chuck Davis, David Fletcher, Chris Hughes, Kelly Kulesza, Greg Ligon, Tony Morgan, Tom Nebel, Russ Olman, Dan Reiland, Chris Ritter, Dale Roach, Kristy Rutter, Jonathan Schaeffer, J. David Schmidt, Daniel Serdahl, Gary Shockley, Wayne Smith, Dave Travis, and Jon S. Vesely.

Finally, thanks to the four-hundred-plus people who took the Leadership Network 2011 survey of church mergers, including those who suggested title ideas along the lines of *Better Together: Making Church Mergers Work*. They include Jeff Butler, Marc Curnutt, Peter DiPippo, Taylor Moffitt, David Rudd, Brad Sargent, and Ildefonso Torres.

Notes

Chapter One: God Is Doing Something New

1. See explanation in Appendix H.
2. See explanation in Appendix H.
3. One Southern Baptist group uses this term. See www.namb .net/namb1pbnewsarchive.aspx?pageid=8589994583.
4. See www.kairoslegacypartners.org.
5. See Warren Bird and Kristin Walters, "Multisite Is Multiplying: Survey Identifies Leading Practices and Confirms New Developments in the Movement's Expansion." Leadership Network, September 2010, p. 9. Retrieved from http://leadnet.org/resources/download/multisite_is_multiplying_ new_developments_in_the_movements_expansion/.
6. The exact figure is that 17 percent of megachurches have merged with another congregation in the previous twenty years. The question was asked in a study jointly conducted by Leadership Network and the Hartford Institute for Religion Research. This particular finding was not mentioned in the overall report about the study, written by Scott Thumma and Warren Bird, "Changes in American Megachurches: Tracing Eight Years of Growth and Innovation in the Nation's Largest-Attendance Congregations," available for free at www.leadnet.org/megachurch.
7. Rick Warren, *The Purpose Driven Church: Growth Without Compromising Your Message and Mission*. Grand Rapids, MI: Zondervan, 1995, 14.

8. This information is based on secondary analysis of the data from FACT 2005 (Faith Communities Today) (http://www .faithcommunitiestoday.org/faith-communities-today-2005-study), much of which is publicly available at ARDA (The Association of Religious Data Archives), www.thearda.com and then in the search box, enter the words *faith communities today*.

9. See http://united.lifechurch.tv.

10. See the website for North Point's strategic partners at www .northpointpartners.org. See also Sheila M. Poole, "North Point Ministries Spreading Its Reach," *Atlanta Journal-Constitution*, Lifestyle section, April 8, 2011. Retrieved from www.ajc.com/ lifestyle/north-point-ministries-spreading-903346.html.

11. See www.multiplicitynetwork.com. The website for New Life Community Church is www.newlifechicago.org.

12. See www.eaglebrookchurch.com/pages/page.asp?page_id=71121.

13. See www.bilcornelius.com/blog/do-you-want-your-church-become-bay-area-fellowship-campus.

14. From personal interview with Dave Travis who referenced Everett Rogers, *Diffusion of Innovations* (5th ed.). New York: The Free Press, 2003, pp. 16, 258, 264.

15. See Scott Thumma and Dave Travis, *Beyond Megachurch Myths: What We Can Learn from America's Largest Churches*. San Francisco: Jossey-Bass, 2007.

16. Lyle E. Schaller, *Growing Plans: Strategies to Increase Your Church's Membership*. Nashville: Abingdon Press, 1983, p. 56.

17. Lyle E. Schaller, *Reflections of a Contrarian*. Nashville: Abingdon Press, 1989, p. 148. See also pp. 141–145.

18. Ibid. See also Chapter Five, "Should We Merge?" in Lyle E. Schaller, *The Small Church Is Different*. Nashville: Abingdon Press, 1982.

Chapter Two: Four Models for Healthy Mergers

1. "Fast Facts." Hartford Institute for Religion Research. Retrieved from http://hirr.hartsem.edu/research/fastfacts/ fast_facts.html#sizecong.

2. http://sundaytown.com/media/restart/. The website for New Life Community Church is www.newlifechicago.org.

3. Richard Laribee, *Factors Contributing to Success or Failure of Congregational Mergers*. Pasadena, CA: Fuller Theological Seminary, 1998, p. 5.

4. Kristen Moulton, "Merger Makes Big Utah Church Even Bigger," *The Salt Lake Tribune*, December 7, 2010. Retrieved from www.sltrib.com/csp/cms/sites/sltrib/pages/printerfriendly .csp?id=50738133.

5. Ibid.

6. "Close Up Interview with Tullian Tchividjian," *Christian Retailing Magazine*, October 2011, p. 22. Retrieved from www.christianretailing.com. See also Tullian Tchividjian, *Jesus Plus Nothing Equals Everything*. Wheaton, IL: Crossway, 2011, pp. 17–23, 194–195.

7. Alice Mann, *Can Our Church Live? Redeveloping Congregations in Decline*. Indianapolis: Alban Institute, 2000, p. 70.

8. Gary L. McIntosh, *Taking Your Church to the Next Level: What Got You Here Won't Get You There*. Grand Rapids, MI: Baker Books, 2009.

9. Thom S. Rainer, *Breakout Churches: Discover How to Make the Leap*. Grand Rapids, MI: Zondervan, 2005, p. 214.

10. Alice Mann, p. 67. See also *Congregational Resource Guide* at http://www.congregationalresources.org/about-crg.

Chapter Three: Missional, Multisite, Multiethnic, and Other Merger Motives

1. See www.kairoslegacypartners.org or http://vimeo.com/ 22086088.

2. Craig Groeschel, "What to Do During Merger Talks," *Swerve*, October 29, 2008. Retrieved from http://swerve.life-church.tv/2008/10/29/what-to-do-during-merger-talks.

3. Shelly Banjo, "Churches Find End Is Nigh: The Number of Religious Facilities Unable to Pay Their Mortgage Is Surging." *Wall Street Journal*, January 24, 2011. Retrieved

from http://online.wsj.com/article/SB100014240527487041
15404576096151214141820.html.
See also Suzanne Sataline, "In Hard Times, Houses of
God Turn to Chapter 11 in Book of Bankruptcy: Strapped
Churches Can't Pay the Mortgage After Borrowing Binge."
Wall Street Journal, November 23, 2008. Retrieved from
http://online.wsj.com/article/SB122999261138328613.html.

4. See David A. Roozen. "Holy Toll: The Impact of the 2008
Recession on American Congregations." Hartford Institute
for Religion Research, April 2011. Retrieved from http://
faithcommunitiestoday.org/sites/faithcommunitiestoday.org/
files/HolyTollReport.pdf.

5. See Warren Bird and Kristin Walters, "Multisite Is
Multiplying: Survey Identifies Leading Practices and
Confirms New Developments in the Movement's Expansion."
Leadership Network, September 2010. Retrieved from http://
leadnet.org/resources/download/multisite_is_multiplying_new_
developments_in_the_movements_expansion/.

6. Story and quotes taken from blog by Tim Stevens, July 19,
2011. Retrieved from www.leadingsmart.com/2011/07/
an-unexpected-gift.html.

7. Warren Bird and Kristin Walters, "Making Multisite
Mergers Work: New Options for Being One Church in Two
or More Locations." Retrieved free from http://leadnet.org/
resources/download/3028.

8. William Vanderbloemen, "Six Trends in Staffing." *Church
Executive*, August 1, 2011. Retrieved from http://churchex
ecutive.com/archives/six-trends-in-staffing.

9. "Churches Join Together," *Ruston Daily Leader*, September
29, 2011. Retrieved from http://www.rustonleader.com/
node/16993.

10. Matthew Wilson, "Can Megachurches Bridge the Racial
Divide?" *Time*, January 11, 2010. Retrieved from www.time
.com/time/magazine/article/0,9171,1950943,00.html.

11. Daniel Rodriguez, *A Future for the Latin Church: Models for Multilingual, Multigenerational Hispanic Congregations*. Downers Grove, IL: InterVarsity Press, 2001.

12. Mark DeYmaz, *Ethnic Blends: Mixing Diversity into Your Local Church*. Grand Rapids, MI: Zondervan, 2010, p. 133.

Chapter Four: Stages and Speed of a Merger

1. John Iwasaki, "Two Very Different Seattle Churches Decide to Unite," *Seattle Post-Intelligencer*, June 3, 2007. Retrieved from www.seattlepi.com/local/article/2-very-different-Seattle-churches-decide-to-unite-1239472.php. See also Pastor Eugene Cho's subsequent blog with updates, http://eugenecho.com/2008/06/02/an-amazing-gift-dying-in-order-to-give-life/

Chapter Five: How to Measure Success

1. Anthony F. Buono and James L. Bowditch, *The Human Side of Mergers and Acquisitions: Managing Collisions Between People, Cultures, and Organizations*. Washington, DC: Beard Books, 1989, p. xiv.

2. Tom Bandy, "The Keys for Successful Church Mergers," 2009. Retrieved from http://dl.dropbox.com/u/33077576/Resources/Articles/Strategic%20Planning/Keys%20for%20Successful%20Church%20Mergers.pdf.

3. David Raymond, "Working with a Collaboration Coach," *Church Collaboration*. Retrieved from www.churchcollaboration.com/Coach.html.

4. Unless otherwise noted, all findings in this paper come from a 2011 Leadership Network survey of churches reported in Warren Bird and Kristin Walters, "Making Multisite Mergers Work: New Options for Being One Church in Two or More Locations." Retrieved free from http://leadnet.org/resources/download/3028.

5. Will Marotti, *America's Best Hope*. Bloomington, IN: Xlibris, 2010, pp. 56–57.

Chapter Six: Why Mergers Fail

1. Tim Donelly, "How to Merge Corporate Cultures." *Inc*, May 9, 2011. Retrieved from www.inc.com/guides/201105/how-to-merge-corporate-cultures.html.
2. William Bridges, *Managing Transitions: Making the Most of Change* (2nd ed.). Cambridge, MA: Perseus, 2003, p. 3.
3. Management Consulting News. "Meet the MasterMinds: William Bridges on Managing Transitions." Retrieved from www.managementconsultingnews.com/interviews/bridges_interview.php.
4. Tom Bandy, "Top Ten Common Pitfalls for Church Mergers." Retrieved from http://dl.dropbox.com/u/33077576/Resources/Articles/Denominations/Top%2010%20Common%20Pitfalls%20for%20Church%20Mergers.pdf. Used with permission.
5. Timothy J. Galpin and Mark Herndon, *The Complete Guide to Mergers and Acquisitions*. San Francisco: Jossey-Bass, 2007, p. 2.
6. Ibid., p. 233.
7. Ibid., p. 5.

Chapter Seven: Financial and Legal Aspects of a Merger

1. Bruce R. Hopkins and David Middlebrook, *Nonprofit Law for Religious Organizations: Essential Questions & Answers*. Hoboken, NJ: John Wiley & Sons, 2008.

Chapter Nine: Determining Whether Your Church Is a Good Merger Candidate

1. See www.redemptionaz.com/about/.
2. Dan Kimball *They Like Jesus but Not the Church*. Grand Rapids, MI: Zondervan, 2007.

Chapter Ten: How to Start the Merger Conversation

1. Geoff Surratt, Greg Ligon, and Warren Bird, A *Multi-Site Church Roadtrip: Exploring the New Normal*. Grand Rapids, MI: Zondervan, 2009, pp. 171–172.

Chapter Eleven: Self-Assessment for Merger Readiness

1. See David Raymond's more detailed explanation at his website www.churchcollaboration.com.
2. A group designed to help churches distribute their property to other ministries is Kairos Legacy Partners at www.legacy churches.com.

Chapter Thirteen: Managing Pain and Change

1. John P. Kotter, *Leading Change*. Boston: Harvard Business Press, 1996. See also a case study of churches: Robert Lewis and Wayne Cordeiro with Warren Bird, *Culture Shift: Transforming Your Church from the Inside Out*. San Francisco: Jossey-Bass, 2005.
2. Samuel R. Chand, *Cracking Your Church's Culture Code: Seven Keys to Unleashing Vision and Inspiration*. San Francisco: Jossey-Bass, 2010.
3. Larry Osborne, *The Unity Factor: Developing a Healthy Church Leadership Team* (4th ed.). Vista, CA: Owl's Nest, 2006.
4. Justin, Anderson, "5 Critical Lessons from a Church Merger," May 22, 2011. Retrieved from http://theresurgence .com/2011/05/22/5-critical-lessons-from-a-church-merger.

Chapter Fourteen: Where Do You Go from Here?

1. Greg Garrison, "Dwindling Pelham Congregation Rebounds After Merger with Megachurch," *The Birmingham News*,

September 3, 2011. Retrieved from http://blog.al.com/living-news/2011/09/dwindling_pelham_congregation.html.
2. Will Mancini, *Church Unique: How Missional Leaders Cast Vision, Capture Culture, and Create Movement.* San Francisco: Jossey-Bass, 2008.
3. Thom S. Rainer and Eric Geiger, *Simple Church: Returning to God's Process for Making Disciples.* Nashville: B&H Publishing, 2011.
4. Geoff Surratt, Greg Ligon, and Warren Bird, *The Multi-Site Church Revolution: Being One Church in Many Locations.* Grand Rapids, MI: Zondervan, 2006.
5. www.census.gov/.
6. http://en.wikipedia.org/wiki/Main_Page.
7. www.uschamber.com/.
8. www.precept.org.

Appendix H: Merger Research

1. Unless otherwise noted, all findings in this paper come from a 2011 Leadership Network survey of churches reported in Warren Bird and Kristin Walters, "Making Multisite Mergers Work: New Options for Being One Church in Two or More Locations." Retrieved free from http://leadnet.org/resources/download/3028.

The Authors

Jim Tomberlin has served the body of Christ in a variety of ministries from pastoring a church in Germany to growing a megachurch in Colorado Springs, to pioneering the multisite strategy at Willow Creek Community Church in Chicago. In 2005, Jim founded MultiSite Solutions, a consulting group to help churches maximize their redemptive potential through intensive and insightful multisite and merger consultation. In this capacity Jim has leveraged his three decades of pastoral experience in navigating numerous churches across the United States through the merger process. He has become one of the leading experts on church mergers with nearly a third of his consulting currently involving merger issues.

Jim resides in Scottsdale, Arizona, and holds a BA in anthropology from Georgia State University in Atlanta and a masters of theology (ThM) from Dallas Theological Seminary. Jim and his wife, Deryl, have three grown children.

Warren Bird, PhD, is director of research and intellectual capital development for Leadership Network. An ordained minister serving on church staff for sixteen years, he now serves as an adjunct faculty member at Alliance Theological Seminary, Nyack, New York. Warren has coauthored twenty-four books, including *Culture Shift: Transforming Your Church from the Inside Out* and *Viral Churches: Helping Church Planters Become Movement Makers*, both from Jossey-Bass.

Index

Page references followed by *fig* indicate an illustrated figure; followed by *t* indicate a table.